8/5

A Crash of Rhinoceroses

To everything there is a season, and
A time to every purpose under heaven

A CRASH OF RHINOCEROSES

A DICTIONARY OF COLLECTIVE NOUNS

Rex Collings

Illustrated by Roderick Booth-Jones

BELLEW PUBLISHING
London
1992

First published in Great Britain in 1992 by
Bellew Publishing Company Ltd
8 Balham Hill
London SW12 9EA

ISBN 0 947792 72 4

Designed by Herman Lelie

Printed and Bound in Great Britain by
Hartnolls Limited, Bodmin, Cornwall.

This work is dedicated to the
memory of
John Hodgkin
and
to my family and friends,
both the living and the dead

ACKNOWLEDGEMENTS

It is not every author who has had the good fortune of having an editor as learned and expert as Mrs McDonald; and I should like here to pay tribute to her for the infinite patience and unfailing good humour that she has shown, but in fairness I must make it clear that the opinions expressed in the text are mine, so too are those balanced judgements that some may, erroneously, label prejudices.

When I was demobilized in 1947, an old family friend paid for my membership of the London Library, without the resources of that marvellous institution and the help and advice of its staff I should never have been able to compile and complete this work.

Finally, I have to thank my friends and family who have with varying degrees of success and unswerving devotion done their best either to write this book for me or, more commonly, to dissuade me from the task, for them my gratitude is unbounded, like a **cast of vultures** they eagerly await the corpse.

CONTENTS

INTRODUCTION

The tradition began with Adam. The author of *Genesis* wrote:

> And out of the ground the Lord God formed every beast
> of the field, and every fowl of the air; and brought
> them unto Adam to see what he would call them.

'And Adam', who was still obedient to God's commands (this was before the unfortunate incident of the spare rib), 'gave names to all cattle, and the fowl of the air, and to every beast of the field'.

From this time man has delighted in finding names for the beasts of the field and the fowls of the air.

This book, or at least the core of it, is concerned with the names that man has given to collections or companies of animals; the terms for a few inanimate objects and some concepts have been included – a 'Basket of Currencies' and a 'Chapter of Accidents' for example – but these are few.

It is a reflection of the English character that often the use of the wrong word or expression was, and sometimes still is, enough to exclude the user from the ranks of 'Gentlemen'; the user was not, as someone once said, 'one of us'. John Betjeman's poem 'How to Get on in Society' makes this point, recording a number of unacceptable words and phrases:

> 'Phone for the fish knives Norman
> As Cook is a little unnerved
> You kiddies have crumpled the serviettes
> And I must have things daintily served.

For would-be sportsmen or sportswomen it could be ruin to speak of 'dogs' rather than 'hounds'; and the male red deer was (and is still) a stag, not a buck* and the female a hind not a doe; and one should never speak of a covey of pheasants nor a gaggle of bantams. Such accuracy – some would call it pedantry – has now almost disappeared; cricket commentators, whom one might have expected to know better, will speak confidently and authoritatively of a batsman as 'third man in' rather than as going in 'first wicket down'.

If, in the past, one had not mastered the special vocabularies, even the most exclusive of old-school ties was not a sufficient guarantee of social acceptablility. Nowadays, such exclusivity survives principally among the young; not to know the latest terms nor performers in the world of pop music may result in banishment from the warm and privileged world of 'us' to the arctic circle of 'them'.

In one of the manuscripts in the British Library which dates from the fifteenth century there is a list of company terms, and a passage that underlines the importance of knowing the right descriptions. It reads:

> Note ye the properteys that longythe to a yonge gentylle man to have knowynge of suche thyngys that longythe unto hym that he fayle not in hys propyr termys that longythe unto hym as hyt shall folowe hereynne wrytynge . . .

Earlier than this, at the close of the thirteenth century, Sir Walter de Bibbesworth wrote a treatise for the instruction of children – a number of different manuscript versions survive. In the section concerning the assembly of beasts, he writes, in Norman French:

---

* In Australia the assembly of males celebrating the forthcoming wedding of one of their number is called a 'bucks party', not as in England a 'stag party'. How did this happen, I wonder; does the term date from the days of Transportation, or is it of more recent origin?

Cher enfaunt, ore entendet
Apres dyner ke cy orrez,
De checune assemble diversement
Vus covent parler proprement.

As one of Sir Walter's editors observed: 'It was an important point of etiquette and good breeding in feudal times to know and apply properly the special term for a company of different animals . . .'

It was not only in feudal times that one finds this obsession with what is right and seemly. Henry Coleman Folkard in *The Wild Fowler* (1859) ends Chapter One with this cannonade against the uninitiated of his times:

There cannot be a stronger proof [of] the ignorance of the present age, as regards the original act of wild-fowling, than by reference to the erroneous terms which are applied to the pursuit by nearly all modern sportsmen; and it is only from the lips of a few 'ancient fowlers', however illiterate, that we hear the correct version of sporting terms applicable to wild-fowling . . . To speak in the present day of a 'flock' of partridges, instead of a 'covey', would so offend the ears of the most superficial sportsman, that he would look upon an individual who made use of such a term with profound pity at his ignorance; and yet the term 'flock' as applied to wild-fowl is equally erroneous, and quite as inexcusable, when coming from the lips of a sportsman . . . Writers upon sporting literature, one and all, commit similar errors . . .

Folkard then lists the correct terms, ancient and modern, and concludes the introductory chapter:

Let us hope the character of the English sportsman is not so far degenerated, or the respect he owes to ancient diversions so far forgotten, as to permit him any longer to persist in such cramped and improper *slang* as to use the inapplicable term 'flock' to every or any description of wild-fowl. It should be borne in mind that as we derive our purest sciences from the ancients, from the same source sprang our national sports; and the rules, the systems, and the terms, in connection with such, have been handed down to us from generation to generation because none express so faithfully the meaning intended to be conveyed.

———

Names are of great importance; they always have been, not only because they separated, socially, the sheep from the goats, but because it used to be thought – indeed in some places it still is – that to know the names of persons or even of things gave one power over them. Some years ago, when I was on holiday in the Hebrides, I was joined on a walk by a red-headed, freckled, small boy; we talked together, rather solemnly, of faraway places, of mountains, and of wild animals. When we reached the croft where he lived, he turned to me and with exquisite natural manners asked me my name. I told him, and then asked him his. He looked at me, then, after a long silence, 'I'm no telling,' he said, 'I'm no telling,' and he stumped away across the field to his home, secure in his anonymity.

The naming of beasts and collections of beasts has from that first bibilical incident fascinated Adam's descendants. When I was a boy we had among our books a battered copy of Dr Brewer's *Dictionary of Phrase and Fable*. It had survived from my mother's childhood, and was much consulted for solving crossword puzzles and settling arguments. In addition to entries on 'The Fathers of the Church' and 'The Lady of Shallott' there was an entry, 'Numbers', under which appeared phrases such as a 'Pride of Lions', a 'Covey of Partridges' and a 'Board of Directors'. The list was not extensive; it did not take up a page of the book. My sister and I, if I remember rightly, used on occasion to make up new phrases for collections of animals and groups of people, sitting on the drawing-room floor after tea on a Sunday, our suggestions growing ever more grotesque and extravagant until my grandmother would say, gently, 'No, darling,' and we would be still.

———

When it was suggested to me that it might be worthwhile producing an annotated list of collective nouns and phrases, I agreed, with some reluctance, to consider the idea. I went first to *Brewer*, the old *Brewer* (the new one does not have an entry on collective nouns), and was disappointed; it did not seem that there was enough material on which to build a book. Later, at the London Library, the Reading Room librarian confirmed my belief (and investigations) that there were in the library no works of reference devoted solely to the listing of collective or company nouns. I found nothing listed in *Books in Print*. I felt frustrated and discouraged; then I remembered Strutt's *Sports and Pastimes*, this I knew contained chapters on hunting and fishing. To my joy, when I consulted my copy, I found lists of hunting terms, terms of venery. One of these lists included such delightful phrases, previously unknown to me, and with little apparent relevance to hunting or indeed fishing, as a 'Blush of Boys', a 'Draught of Butlers' and a 'Temperance of Cooks'.

Further investigations produced a number of sporting books that contained glossaries of specialized terms; and one of the librarians drew my attention to Hellweg's *Weird and*

Wonderful Words, the short list in which included a 'Crash of Rhinoceroses' and a 'Pod of Whales'. In my memory, too, I carried locked away a faint recollection that somewhere I had seen mentioned a reprint of one of those early-medieval treatises on hunting that had been issued in one of their collections by a learned society in the nineteenth century. I searched the shelves, at first in vain; it was only when I began checking those descriptions that I had already noted, in the *OED*, that I came across a reference to *The Booke of St Albans*. This was a marvellous find. There was a copy in the library, and this led me to a paper that a certain scholarly member, John Hodgkin, had presented to the Philological Society in 1907 and which was printed in a volume of their *Transactions*. Here was just what I had been searching for; and here too was learning, wit and scholarship. Not only was the list from *The Booke of St Albans* reprinted, but also other lists collected from medieval manuscripts, *incunabula*, and later Tudor and Stuart books. Here was the base on which to build. This is why I have thought it appropriate to dedicate this book to the memory of Mr Hodgkin.

During my searches I discovered that Britain's second greatest lexicographer, J A H Murray, the compiler of the *Oxford English Dictionary*, wrote to *Notes & Queries* – the letter was published in the 7 November 1888 issue – asking:

> Where can I find a list of the technical terms, such as pair, brace, couple, etc., applied in sporting language to different species of animals; or any names applied to herds, droves, flocks, or collections of animals? I know, of course, the list in the *Book of St Albans* of 'The compaynys of beestys and fowlys' containing among other fifteenth century beasts and fowls 'a Herde of harlotys', 'a Bevy of Ladies', 'a superfluyte of Nunnys', 'a sculke of freris', 'a bhomynable sight of monkis'; but I

want a reference something more recent and practical.
Answer direct.

J A H Murray   The Scriptorium, Oxford

It was perhaps unfortunate that Murray had added 'Answer
direct' to his letter for only one letter was published in
answer to his inquiry, and this refers him to the lists in
Randle Holme's *Academy of Armory and Blazon*, 1688.

Ten years later, however, in the 3 August 1895 issue of
Notes & Queries, S James A Salter of Basingstoke lists seven
company terms for birds, and asks:

> Can these be added to? . . . These assemblages of birds
> are at first confined each to a single family; but as the
> season advances they merge and combine, especially
> where sportsmen have been at work . . . I have shot the
> common widgeon, the pochard, and the pintail out of the
> same knob.

This letter produced a number of answers, including one
from E Cobham Brewer who wrote: 'Perhaps I may escape
censure if I suggest that on p.901, Col 2, of the new edition
of *Phrase and Fable*, nearly ten times seven are mentioned';
and one from California suggested: 'to the seven names of
groups of birds mentioned might be added that of a gang of
wild turkeys as used by old hunters in our Western States.'
This and a number of the other letters are particularly
interesting because they seem to reflect what terms were
actually being used, so many of the sources, like the ones in
Strutt, are simply lists.

It was much later, when my collection was nearly ready,
that I was sent from America a copy of *An Exaltation of
Larks*, an American-oriented book by James Lipton, who
also makes great use of *Hodgkin* and Dame Juliana Barnes's
Booke of St Albans; but Lipton has not provided the sources

nor any explanations for many of the terms he includes on his lists. His book, however, is the most comprehensive that I have seen.

It was difficult to decide how to present the terms. A straight alphabetical order for the list of subjects was not really the answer; something more attractive was needed. I have therefore chosen to list the collective nouns alphabetically and used the index for listing the subjects. A complete list is almost impossible – a select one is the only reasonable solution – but selection is in itself an onerous task; should I, as a loyal former gunner, champion the inclusion of a 'Troop or Battery of Guns'? Or indeed a 'Battery of Chickens'? *Brewer* lists 'Army' as a company word, which it is, but so too is 'School' and 'Class' and 'Eleven'. What criteria other than or in addition to personal choice have I adopted?

First, the terms listed by Hodgkin are included but not in all the divers forms in which they appear. There is only one entry for a 'Herd of Deer' although there are a number of variants recorded by him. These variants include 'Herde', 'Heard' and 'Hearde', being the forms in which they appear in some of the sources. Then, later, more modern terms, including a 'Pod of Whales' and a 'Crash of Rhinoceroses' and a 'Basket of Currencies' are defined; but not – although our old *Brewer* did – a 'House of Senators' or a 'Suit of Clothes'.

Then, where animals are concerned, I have tried to be as inclusive as possible, but in other cases exclusion has had to be rather drastic, which is in some ways a pity, for quite often one notices in a book a phrase that clearly invents a new collective term. For example, in a collection of short stories by Margery Allingham a character compares a group of tiresome gossiping people to a 'Convocation of Lay Readers' and a novel by the same author was entitled *A Clutch of Constables*. Another novel I saw recently was entitled *A Confederacy of Dunces*, a term that I had not encountered before, although this appeared in a newspaper article in March 1992. Because I remember the excitement and tension at the time of Dunkirk, I have included an 'Armada of Small Ships', but this is not only for the sake of piety; 'Armada' is now quite widely used to describe any collection of ships.

It is interesting that few of the terms are, in origin at least, general or comprehensive; a 'Covey of Partridges' referred originally to a brood, one family, not to all the partridges that might be feeding together; a 'Kennel of Hounds' to a particular 'Pack of Hounds'. Investigation shows that in the early sources the terms were particular. *The Booke of St Albans* says: 'Twelve make a sounder of wild swine. Sixteen a middle sounder and twenty or more a great sounder.' The English of these early sources is simple, direct and unambiguous, reflecting what some – but not I – would claim to be the bluff, honest straightforwardness of the countryman unspoiled by the affectation of courtly life.

One of the unexpected and enjoyable pleasures of my task has been the discovery of new words and expressions; the explorations of sources; in Lean's *Collectanea*, a wonderful chrestomathy of folklore, proverbs, saws and inconsequential facts, there is this description: 'he looks like a cow's turd stuck with primroses'. Who 'he' was is not disclosed, but what better or more accurate description of one of those garden-party or Ascot hats could one find if one only substitutes 'it' for 'he': economical, direct and fair. To adjust one's language to modern convention one might, depending on the company, bow to Mrs Grundy and substitute 'cowpat' for 'cow's turd', but to do so would lessen the shock without diminishing the offence.

———

Shortly before the 1990 Frankfurt Book Fair, I was tele-
phoned by the designer of this book and told that he wanted,
at once, half a dozen or so descriptions or specimen entries
so that he could prepare the dummy for the publisher to
show at the fair. I protested; I had then neither notes nor
books with me, but he was insistent and I was obliged to
invent definitions: being after luncheon the entries I prepared tended to be on the lighter side. This led to complica-
tions, for when these were shown to an American publisher
they so entranced his wife that for a terrifying moment (if
American co-operation were to be achieved) it seemed that I
should have to change my approach and invent all the
definitions. Being a humorist neither by inclination nor
training, however, I managed to wrest the idea back to the
original plan. I will quote three of the descriptions that were
the cause of the problem:

A Crash of Rhinoceroses: 'My God,' Carruthers
exclaimed and leapt from the Jeep.'Here comes a crash of
rhinoceroses.' But it was too late; he was flattened, poor
old fellow.

Memoirs of an Old Shikari

A Blush of Boys: His Eminence Peter Cardinal
Nightingale paused as he entered the Choir. The white of
the boys surplices palely reflected the richness of his
purple robes. 'Charming,' he murmured, 'quite charming, a blush of boys.'

A Non-patience of Wives: In the glen the clan gathered,
the men resplendent in their kilts, marshalled and
apparelled for war, the women wailing and weeping,
mouthing Gaelic obscenities. The Clan Chief, affection-
ately called Traigh Mohr, roared to his steward: 'Awa'
with them, awa' with them, that non-patience of wives.'

From The McColls' Lament

There have been – for language is forever changing, extending and retracting its vocabulary – new collective nouns being coined and old ones disappearing since the days when the list in *The Booke of St Albans* was first compiled; and the meanings of words, too, have changed as the years have passed. It is amazing how original descriptions and definitions have altered. Consider, for example, a 'Temperance of Cooks'. This phrase, until I read it in *Strutt*, I had neither read nor heard before. It conjured up pleasant visions of past ages. One vision I had might have been recorded in a volume of those delightful and nostalgic *Memoirs* of a childhood spent in the splendid affluence of the early, golden, years of this century, when the sun always shone in summer and all young men (if family photograph albums are to be believed) looked – even if they did not behave – like Rupert Brooke, and girls were doe-eyed, lovely and fresh as the lilies-of-the-valley, dormant volcanoes, like Lucy waiting to erupt at the first illicit kiss. I wrote such a description:

> I well remember, wrote the diarist, my great aunt observing to my mother on the occasion of the Coronation of George V, when the cooks from the big houses had been sent to prepare the celebration feast for the whole village, 'Eleanor, my dear, we may be exhorted not to muzzle the stalled ox, but please go and tell Tompkins to remove the cask of Sherry wine, the amount that temperance of cooks has consumed would have been enough to make trifle for the whole of Lord Kitchener's army.'

In fact 'Temperance' is a corruption of 'Tempering', which meant: 'mixing with liquid flavourings such as vinegar, verjuice, wine and water, or milk of almonds'. *Hodgkin* suggests that it may refer to 'a heavy hand in seasoning, an ill-judged excess'.

Terms, specialist terms, exist not only for groups of beasts and people. *Cox* lists 'Terms of Copulayion': a boar 'goeth to brim', while a fox 'goeth to clicketting'. These terms have now fallen into desuetude, being replaced by new ones such as 'bonking', a sporting term which was, I believe, popularized some years ago in tennis circles.

There is in a manuscript* dating from the fifteenth century, a poem describing animal noises:

> At my hose I have a jaye
> He can make any diverse leye;
> He can barkying as a foxe,
> He can lowe as a noxe
> He can crecun as a gos
> He can romy as a nasse in his cracke,
> He can croden as a froge,
> He can barkun as a dogge
> He can cheteron as a wrenne,
> He can cokelyn as a henne,
> He canne neye as a stede,
> Such a byrde were wode to fede.

There is no reason why new terms should not be invented (as 'bonking' demonstrates), new phrases coined; sports and pastimes have changed, so too have occupations. Language is living, vibrant, and it reflects the lives and aspirations of those who use it. Dictionaries are brought up to date, lexicographers search and mine newspapers and books for new words and usages. As Don Cupitt wrote in *Creation Out of Nothing:* 'Articulacy is power. Your vocabulary shapes your world for you and enables you to get a grip on it.' The way in which words and phrases are used often reflects not

---

* Harl. No 1002 Fol. 72, recto.

only the individual attitudes and prejudices of the user, but prevailing national attitudes and fashions as well.

In the medieval lists of company terms which date mostly from the fifteenth to the early sixteenth century, the fierce anti-clericalism of the times can be detected quite easily. John Wyclif, the inspirer of the Lollards, died in 1384 and it was he who gave intellectual backing and respectability to the widespread dissatisfaction that had generally arisen among laymen with the Church's dignitaries and their flamboyant and extravagant lifestyle. Chaucer (died 1400) exhibits this adverse critical view of the clergy in his portrayal of pilgrims like the Pardoner, the Friar and the Monk, although he does in contrast praise the poor Parson. In the lists we therefore find a 'Skulk of Friars', a 'Superfluity of Nuns', an 'Abominable Sight of Monks' and a 'Lying of Pardoners'.

————

We are sensitive, perhaps overly so, to the accusation of being racist or sexist. The contemptuous references, sometimes merely asides, to Jews and members of the black races which were common before the war and which disfigure the works and often spoil our enjoyment of writers of the calibre of Buchan and Chesterton are not acceptable today. The assumptions that all Jewish financiers tend to be shady or crooked and all Black people tend to be of limited intelligence are no longer made, although, if not in print, the Irish are still considered by some to be rather on the thick side and in Australia an Englishman may expect to be called 'a brimming whinging Pom' – I substitute one of those old hunting terms for the normal word which the limited-vocabularied occupants of the Hill would normally use.

An interesting example of the medieval Englishman's

racist attitude towards the Scots is shown in the term a 'Disworship of Scots'. For the English, the Scots were a squalid nuisance, always raiding, raping and ravening; indulging in piracy and frequently obsequiously seeking subsidies, especially when England was at war with France; and, at least according to English interpretations, prone to treaty bending and breaking and general dissimulation and deceit.

————

Seeing and being part of a group of publishers at the Frankfurt Book Fair clustered round the various bars, gossiping, plotting, wheeler-dealing, chattering, I searched my mind desperately for a word or phrase that would accurately describe their corporate identity. What could one use? A 'Temperance' would be wildly inaccurate, a 'Blush' improbable, a 'Gaggle', almost, but too feminine, a 'Giggle' too camp. Finally the answer came: a 'Pod'. It *sounds* right, and the equation of publishers to killer or even sperm whales thrashing about in the ocean seeking victims to devour has much to commend it. Yes, a 'Pod of Publishers'; not at all bad! But the reader may quite legitimately prefer some other term, if so there is no reason why he or she should not invent their own description, for it is pleasant and not too difficult to coin new phrases. A 'Smut of Pornographers' is my publisher's contribution, for example; but the satisfactory and fascinating experience is to find new phrases or variations and adaptations of old ones in print or in use.

The phrase used as the title of this book, which I saw first in *Hellweg*, a 'Crash of Rhinoceroses', is recorded in *Lipton* as having been used in one of the reports of the Kenya Game Department. It is established thereby as a genuine term, even though it may not be universally accepted at present by zoologists as the legitimate term for a gathering or company of rhinoceroses. There is, however, no reason why in time it should not be, even as a 'Pride of Lions' or a 'Pod of Whales' eventually achieved lexicographical respectablility.

To discover the old lists of company names is, and was, very satisfying; but it is much more exciting to find these terms used in contemporary works. How exciting it would be if one of the readers of this book could find some book or manuscript in which terms like a 'Blush of Boys' or a 'Non-patience of Wives' were actually used.

Old terms become obsolete and atrophy, to be rescued for crossword puzzles and general-knowledge tests and quizzes. It is unlikely that one will find in the contemporary novel or indeed in other works many of the terms listed in this book. It is true, as I have recorded, that I heard a naturalist on a BBC programme refer to a 'Pod of Whales' and Ruth Rendell calls one of her many detective stories *An Unkindness of Ravens*, but such examples are few. The usual place in which terms do occur are in the quiz shows; on one of these I heard recently the question: 'What is a collection of bears called?' The competitor failed to give the right answer; it should have been 'Sloth'. There are terms that are in common use: a 'Flock of Sheep', a 'Covey of Partridges', and a 'Gaggle of Geese'. Those of us fortunate enough to have been nurtured on *The Book of Common Prayer* and the neglected service of Matins can and do remember with pleasure and nostalgia the thunderous affirmations of the 'Noble Army of Martyrs', the 'Goodly Fellowship of the Prophets' and the 'Glorious Company of the Apostles' – one wonders whether this last description was ever used of the Cambridge Apostles?

At a stretch one could – and I do – include in the list a 'Pool of Typists'; visions of beautiful if somewhat scantily clad young persons disporting themselves in some subterranean swimming pool waiting for the summons from upstairs is a delicious one, delicious of course if one is interested in that kind of thing: but alas this pool is of another construction. The poets, if one is prepared to twist the words, can provide examples too. Blake's 'The tigers of wrath are wiser than the horses of instruction' could give us a 'Wrath of Tigers' and an 'Instruction of Horses' – both have a nice feel to them, but this is fantasy rather than reality, although Wordsworth has given us '... a crowd/A host of golden daffodils'. And the modern poet Tony Harrison told me that when the rehearsals for his play *Trackers* were taking place at the National Theatre in 1990, the designer wanted a collective noun to describe the monstrous phalluses with which the chorus, following Greek tradition, had been endowed. After much deliberation the word chosen was 'Clutch'. What earnest researcher or dictionary compiler will in the future, while hot in pursuit of a doctorate, seek to discover where and when the phrase a 'Clutch of Phalluses' was first used?*

It is a delight to find new phrases, and we have left a few blank pages at the book's end for you, the reader, to use to record discoveries of your own, not only of new phrases from the books and papers you read and the broadcasts and television programmes you hear and watch, but also of examples of the use of the ones listed that you may have found in those old books that you read: in the works of Dickens, Jane Austen, Fielding or Thomas Browne, or going further back still, in Chaucer or Langland.

I shall end, echoing George Turbervile from his *Noble Arte of Venerie or Hunting* (1576): 'Therefore I have thought my parte to set down such as I myselfe have eyther herd pronounced by olde Huntesmen, or found approved in old Trystrams booke.'

---

* Since this was written, I read in Brian Aldiss: *The Hand-Reared Boy* (London, 1970): 'A clutch of penises was the agreed collective noun.'

THE COLLECTIVE NOUNS

An Abominable Sight of Monks

An Abominable Sight of Monks

The medieval lists are shot through with a marked antipathy to the Religious. How widespread this dislike was is at this distance difficult to determine, but it is present in Chaucer and Langland, and the Lollards and Wyclif exhibit this dislike very strongly at the national level. It is not therefore surprising to find it reflected in the contemporary lists.

An **abominable sight of monks** and the complementary a **superfluity of nuns** are said to replace the earlier a **devoutness of monks** and an **holiness of nuns**.

Somewhere, not long ago, I heard a tired and slightly inebriated guest at an official dinner complain of the **super-fluity of toasts** – it was the rambling, incomprehensible introductory speeches that seemed unnecessary and super-fluous not the actual **toasts**. One early eighteenth-century **toast** that rather appeals to me is:

May times mend and down with the bloody Brunswicks.

Different from the Orange toast which is printed in one of Hone's sixpenny pamphlets.* The text of the toast appears in a footnote:

This loyal toast, handed down by Orange tradition, is literally as follows; we give it for the edification of the English reader:

The glorious, pious, and immortal memory of the great and good King William, who saved us from Pope and Popery, James and slavery, brass money and wooden shoes. Here is bad luck to the Pope, and a hempen rope to all Papists.

It is drank kneeling, if they cannot stand, nine times nine; amid various mysteries which none but the *elect* can comprehend.

* *The Eloquent Speech of Charles Phillips. Esq. At Galway, in the case of O'Mullan v. M'Korkill*, 1816.

Lean records a saying from 1642: 'As odious as **monks** and **friars**'. For **friars** see under **skulk**.

An Armada of Ships

Most English children know (or at least they should) the story of the destruction of the Spanish **Armada** (1588), that fleet which had been so carefully assembled to carry the vast invasion army of Philip II which was to liberate England from the Protestant despotism of Elizabeth. The **Armada** was destroyed as the victory medal records by 'God, who', after Drake had finished his game of bowls at Plymouth, 'blew and they were scattered'.

The term **armada** is now widely used for any collection of **ships** whether large or small: 'A small **armada of merchant ships** – mainly roll on roll off car ferries – is being assembled by the US to reinforce its forces in the Gulf' ([London] *Evening Standard*, 22 November 1990).

In the *Sunday Telegraph* of 27 January 1991 an article on the Gulf War began: 'This weekend 20,000 US marines are aboard an **armada of assault ships** in the Gulf . . .'

Armada is derived from the latin *armare:* to arm. **Fleet** is another term often used of ships, for Sunday 3 January 171¾, *The Political State*, Vol VII, has: 'A **fleet of guarantees** was seen this day off Dover.'

In *Punch*, 25 November 1931, in the 'Essence of Parliament' there was a caricature of Mr Hore Belisha, its caption read:

El Draco of Devonport [his constituency] defies
the **Armada of Abnormal Importations**.

Army

One tends to think of **army** or **armies** as the organized collection or assembly of soldiers: witness 'The Eighth Army' or Napoleon's 'Grande Armee'. But **army** can be used, and is indeed used, for almost any large organized

An Armada of Ships

collection of people. An **army of workmen**, the '**Noble Army of Martyrs**' (from the *Te Deum*) or an **army of washerwomen**.

The [London] *Evening Standard*, 31 January 1991, reporting the closure of a popular West End wine bar, said: 'Its **army of regulars** . . . include an odd mix of senior civil servants, and company directors . . .'

The Booke of St Albans has an **army of soldiers**, and *Grant* has an **army of ghosts,** and Bishop Hall (see **drift**): **armies of frogs** and **caterpillars**.

An Atlas of Maps

There are all kinds and manner of **atlases**; groups of charts and diagrams of the body when collected together and published are often called an **atlas**. In *Books in Print* one finds: An **atlas of anatomy**.

Why **atlas**? Atlas was the legendary king of Mauretania who bore the world on his shoulders; one of the first collection of maps by Mercator had the figure of Atlas on the title page; hence the name for a **collection of maps**.

A Badelyng of Ducks

An obsolete term for a **brood of ducks**. It appears in *Strutt* and the early sources.

Hellweg has a **paddling of ducks**.

In *Notes & Queries 2*, Mr Stilwell lists a **badelynge of ducks** and Mr Parish a **paddling of ducks** in the water. *Folkard* has: 'I had detected, by sound, a fine **paddling of ducks**, feeding in a small bay, the shore of which was skirted by a thick copse . . .'

A Bale of Straw

Chambers defines **bale** as: 'a bundle or package of goods: the set of dice for any special game (obs.).' **Bale of straw, bale**

of wool are today in common use. In Scott's *Fortunes of Nigel* the following quotation can be found: '"Marry, thou hast me on the hip there, thou miserly cony-catcher," answered the Captain, taking a **bale of dice** from the sleeve of his coat.'

The **bale** or **set of dice** usually consisted of three pieces. In *Toone*, in the definition of a **bale of dice**, a quotation from Ben Jonson's *New Inn* is given: 'For exercise of arms a **bale of dice**.'

Band

Chambers' definition is: 'a number of persons bound together for any common purpose . . . a herd or flock?'

Henry V, at least according to Shakespeare, declaimed before Agincourt:

> We few, we happy few, we **band of brothers**
> For he to-day that sheds his blood with me
> Shall be my **brother** . . .

John Mason Neale, the hymn writer, in two of his hymns has:

> O happy **band of pilgrims**

in the one, and

> Around the throne of God a **band**
> **of Glorious Angels** always stand

in the other.

A Barren of Mules

The *OED* has: 'Specific term for a **drove of mules**'. It may be that as *Hodgkin* suggests this is a corruption of the word **berynge** (bearing) and is a *double entendre* suggested by the barrenness of the mule. The Latin for the offspring of a

A Basket of Currencies

stallion and she-ass is a *burdo* – in English, a **hinny**; a **mule** is the result of crossing a jackass with a mare. In Latin America and in some US States, Florida for example, the ass is called a **burro**.

Peacham (1636) has: 'for said Cosmo the excellence of rare spirits are heavenly formes, and no **burthen-bearing mules**'. According to *Wright*, a **barren** was 'a heifer cow or sheep that had ceased to breed', he goes on to quote the case where 'three **barrens** were seized for tithes'.

In *Coningsby* Disraeli wrote: 'It seems to me a **barren** thing this Conservatism – an unhappy cross-breed, the **mule** of politics that engenders nothing.' It does not appear that much has changed.

A Basket of Currencies
When referring to the value of the pound sterling, the BBC reports often gave it against a **basket of currencies**, that is against a number of different, usually European, currencies. This was before the then Tory Government's craven surrender to European pressure, joining the ERM (Exchange Rate Mechanism) and becoming the poodle of German bankers and Brussels bureaucrats.

A Batch of Bread
'The quantity', says *Elworthy*, 'baked at one time'. He quotes *Palsgrave*: '**Batche of bread**, *fournee de pain*.' See also **cast**.

The Bench of Bishops
The **Bench of Bishops** originally referred to the bishops sitting in their capacity as Lords spiritual on their **bench** in the House of Lords; old prints of Parliament show members sitting on plain wooden **benches**. The term now is loosely and inaccurately used to describe *all* the diocesan and

suffragan bishops of the Church of England. All diocesans do not sit in the House of Lords; since the Reformation there has been a **multiplying of bishops** (see **husbands**), the system producing them seems as fecund as rabbits, or white mice, quality frequently being sacrificed to quantity.

In Parliament, leading members of the Government and the Opposition are quite often referred to as front-**bench** spokesmen.

The **Bench** is also used collectively to describe the **judges** and **magistrates**. Members of the governing bodies of the Inns of Court are called **benchers**.

An example of a new term appeared in *The Times*, 20 February 1992, p. 16. The Religion Correspondent wrote:

> An unofficial decree went out from the Church of England yesterday; the collective noun for a group of bishops is a **bully**. The title was granted after bishops, attending yesterday's General Synod, exchanged their purple cassocks for pink tracksuits and their croziers for hockey sticks to take on the blue-troused Mothers' Union at hockey.

The bishops won 2 nil. Personally I doubt that this term will survive. It is too true a description of a number of the present **bench** to be acceptable by the Establishment.

Eric Partridge, in *Slang, Today and Yesterday* (1970), quotes Professor Wyld: '. . . No man who is not a fool will consider it proper to address a **bevy of Bishops** [*nor, I think*, comments Partridge, *would he – unless in his cups – call a group of bishops a **bevy**; a **bevy of partridges**, perhaps, but hardly **of prelates***] in precisely the same way as would be perfectly natural and suitable among a party of fox-hunting country gentlemen.'

A Berry of Holes

Elworthy records this term: 'A group of rabbit holes having internal communications. Called also a **berry of holes** . . . applied equally to the "earths" or holes of **foxes** and **badgers**; never applied to a single hole.'

In a short story, *The Man* by T H White, a man and a boy are going rabbit-shooting, the man speaks to the boy: 'We'll try the **bury** on Huggett's side,' he says.

Bevy

The *OED* says that **bevy** is the proper term for a company of **maidens** or **ladies**, of **roes**, of **quails**, or of **larks**.

Both *Wright* and *Halliwell* include this transcription from a fifteenth-century manuscript:

> How many **herdes** be there of bestes of venery?
> Sire, of **hertis**, of **bisses**, of **bukkes**, and of **doos**.
> A **soundre of wylde swyne**. A **bevy of roos**.

In this quotation 'bisses' is a form of the french word **biche**, the female of the **hart**.

Gent records: **Bevy**: A company of **roes, quails**, etc. *Webster* as an example quotes from *Beaumont & Fletcher* (no specific play named): 'What a **bevy** of beaten **slaves** have we here?'

A Blast of Hunters

The rules governing the occasions when the **huntsmen** could blow their horns were very carefully laid down. It is not clear, however, whether the **hunters** are those taking part in the 'Hunt' or the **huntsmen**, the servants of the **hunt**. Nowadays **hunt** usually refers to all members and the **Hunts** are differentiated by a local name – for example, The Quorn.

A Blush of Boys

A Blush of Boys

Alas, an obsolete term for a company of boys. The description appears in *The Booke of St Albans* and in several other of the early sources, but outside these lists I have not been successful in finding where it was used. It seems a great pity that such a phrase should be so little known and used. It would make an admirable title for one of those novels that hovers indecisively on the edge of pornography. *Lean* has two sayings, undated, 'To blush like a black dog' and 'He blushes like a red bull-calf'. Neither of these has much to do with boys.

Evans & Evans (1881): in the section on proverbs this note appears: 'The phrase was once casually used in my hearing, and I was moved to ask when it was that the red bull-calf had blushed? "A nivver blooshed but wanst," said Sam, "an that wur laast Moonday wur a wik, when Kimberlin's mule called 'im 'bahsta'd'".'

In a long poem called 'Christmas', published in Bristol in 1795, the following lines occur:

> . . . which soon together brought
> A **tribe of boys**, who thund'ring at the doors
> Of those, their fellows, sunk in Somnus' arms,
> Great hubbub made, and much the town alarm'd.

See also Introduction, p.24

Board

A **board of governors**, a **board of trustees** and a **board of directors** (this is in *Brewer*). These are specialist terms relating to special bodies: an individual school or trust, a particular company. The derivation is simple; it comes from a group of people sitting round a table. The governing bodies of the University Presses differ: they are not the **board**; for Oxford they are the **Delegates** and Cambridge the **Syndics**.

In a cathedral, the governing body is the **chapter** and for the United Kingdom the **Parliament**, or more properly perhaps the **Crown in Parliament**. So, of course, one could go on; many institutions and organizations have special terms for their sovereign body.

A Bottle of Hay

Bottle is a term found in many dialects. It is an old word for a **bundle**. In *Jackson*:

> A thousand pounds, and a **bottle of hay**
> Is all one thing at Doom's-day

which is from Howell's *Proverbs* (1660).

He goes on to quote Chaucer: 'Al-though it be nat worth a **botel hay**', and Shakespeare (*A Midsummer Night's Dream*): 'I have a great desire to a **bottle of hay**'. 'In Norfolk', *Jackson* says, 'it denotes the quantity of **hay** that may serve for one feed.'

Peacock records: 'That no man shall get anie **bottells of furres [furze]** and to pay for every that is gotten iiijd' from *Scottes Manor Roll* (1578); and also, 'Will Lee, of Northallerton, for stealing a **bottle of hay**'. 1621. *Quarter Sessions Records*, North Riding Record Society.

There is a Somerset saying: 'One may as well search for a needle in a **bottle of hay**.' *Elworthy* also quotes this saying, but has **straw** in place of **hay**, and he also refers to a **burden of straw**, that is, 'as much as a man can carry on his back'.

Bouquet

Those who profess an exquisite appreciation of fine wines will often talk of the **bouquet**, by which they mean the smell of the wine released when it is poured into a glass and 'breathes'. More commonly, **bouquet** is used of bunches of **flowers** or **herbs** – a **bouquet of roses**, a **wedding bouquet**;

Bouquet

a bunch of aromatic herbs is called a **bouquet garni**. The term has also been used of **pheasants**. This is noted in *British Sports*. 'It is', says the author, 'the flight of a number of **pheasants** breaking cover from the central point at which the beaters meet. This centre point itself.'

Another use is recorded in the despatch from Italy printed in *The Times*, 2 June 1879. Describing celebrations in Rome the reporter writes: 'In the evening that marvel of fireworks the *Girandola* was given from the Castle St Angelo, the great **bouquet of rockets** being particularly fine.'

A recipe in *The Sunday Times*, 16 December 1990, was headed **Bouquet of Vegetables**; this consisted of new potatoes, cauliflower, courgettes, and mangetouts, but could no doubt include other vegetables.

A Brace of Greyhounds

A **brace** is two, but of **hounds; foxhounds,** two form a **couple**, although some early sources do list a **brace of hounds**. A **pack of hounds** is numbered in couples.

In the 1520s, the young James V of Scotland wrote a letter of thanks to his cousin, the bastard Henry Fitzroy, Duke of Richmond, for the 'two **brace of hounds** for deer and smaller beasts' he had sent him.

Spaniels and **harriers** operate in **couples**, see a **cast of hawks**.

Three **greyhounds** make a **lease** and so, too, do three **hawks**. These terms appear in many of the books on hunting and falconry.

Strutt records that: 'Edward the Third . . . has with him in his Army sixty **couple of staghounds**' and also quotes the line from the poem 'Squyer of lowe degree':

A **lese of her hounds** with **her** to strake.

The harehound is another name for the greyhound. In a note emphasizing King John's partiality to greyhounds: *1 palfrido velouter currente et 2 laissius leporariorum* is translated: one swift running horse and six greyhounds. (*Strutt*)

Whitehead has a **relay of hounds**, that is two or three **couples**. *The Master of Game* in the notes has: '**Limer, lymer**, a name given to a scenting-hound which was held in a **liam** or **leash** whilst tracking the games. **Limers** never were a distinct breed of hounds.' Also under **relay**: 'After the **stag** has been started from his lair by a **limer**, some hounds were uncoupled and laid on, the rest being divided off into **relays** . . . there were usually three **relays**, and two to four **couples** the usual number in each **relay**.'

Northall defines 'the shape of a good greyhound'.

A head like a snake, a neck like a drake
A back like a beam, a belly like a bream,
A foot like a cat, a tail like a rat.

In *Daniel*, Vol I: 'In December 1794, a **company of Gentlemen** were coursing at Finchingfield, in Essex, a hare was started, and a **brace of greyhounds** in running at her, ran against each other, and were both killed on the spot.'

Pheasants are often sold as a **brace** – a cock and a hen.

Cox in his list has:

A **Brace** or **Lease of Bucks**.
A **Brace** or **Lease of Foxes**.
A **Brace** or **Lease of Hares**.

and

A **Couple of Rabbits**.
A **Couple of Coneys**.

Earlier *Cox* records: 'The **Coney** is called the first year a **Rabbit**, and afterwards an old **Coney**.' *Elworthy* for **couple** has: 'An ewe and her lamb. A **double couple** is an ewe with two lambs.'

On Farming Today (BBC Radio 4) on 7 March 1992, I heard an old Cornish farmer say that he was going to an auction to watch prices of 'sheep **couples**, that's ewe and lambs . . .'

A Brood of Hens

A **brood**: a family of young hatched at one time, a **hatch**. This is the *OED* definition and is analogous to a **covey of partridges** or an **eye of pheasants**.

Today one would talk of a **flock of chickens** or of one of those monstrous and unpleasant innovations: a **battery of chickens**.

In some of the early sources there is a **peep of chickens**, based on the noise that the chickens make.

Mr Blenkinsopp in *Notes & Queries 2* includes in his list a **brood of grouse** and **black game**.

A Building of Rooks

Building, perhaps because of the time and energy spent by **rooks** when constructing and maintaining their nests. It is found in *Strutt* and in the earlier medieval sources. The use survives: 'Everyone', according to the *Standard* of 26 September 1883, 'with any pretence to be gentle-folk spoke of a **building of rooks**.'

In Richard Jefferies's *Wood Magic* (1881) it is the **Council of Rooks** which provides the disciplined organized force that plays so important a part in the defeat of the invading imperial hordes of pigeons.

Lydgate has a **byldyn of rooks**; *Chambers*, a **clamour of rooks** and so does *Hellweg*. Mr Parish in his *Notes & Queries 2* list has a **wing** or **congregation of plover** or **rooks**. He also includes a **shoal of rooks**. 'Stonehenge', otherwise J H Walsh in *British Rural Sports*, a book which went through many

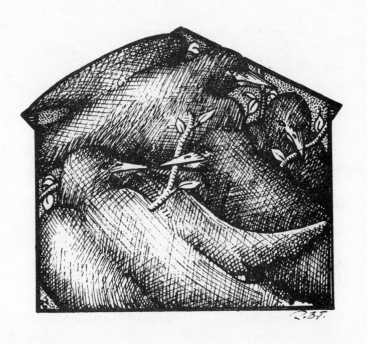

A Building of Rooks

editions, confirms this for **plover** but makes no mention of **rooks**.

The entry in Montagu's *Ornithological Dictionary of British Birds* (1833) contains an anecdote about the rookery in Doctors' Commons:

> Some years ago there were several large elm-trees in the college garden . . . in which a number of Rooks had taken up their abode, forming, in appearance, a sort of **convocation of aerial ecclesiastics**. A young gentleman, who lodged in an attic, and was their close neighbour, frequently entertained himself with thinning this **covey of black game** by means of a crossbow.

A misuse of **covey** and of **black game** – and he a colonel!

Bunch

A general term, used of many divers objects.

Drayton, Song XXV, has:

> And neere to them ye see the lesser dibling **Teale**
> In **Bunches**, with the first that flie from Mere to Mere.

In the margin is a note for **Bunch**: the word in falconry for a company of **teale**.

In *The Athenaeum* No. 240 of 1832, there is a review of an exhibition of pictures at Somerset House; a painting by Uwins, 'The Saint Manufactory', is thus described: '. . . an artist's shop where Madonnas, saints, angels, are manufactured; two friars are bargaining for a **bunch of cherubs**.'

And Herschel in a lecture speaks of 'That comet . . . was a mere **bunch of vapours**.' Compare this with Hamlet's '**congregation of vapours**'.

Of **duck**, E Jesse in *Gleanings in Natural History*, Series III, p.146, has: 'They came in what are called **bunches** . . . sometimes 150 in a **bunch**.'

Whitehead records that **bunch** is a West Country term for a **mob of deer**.

A Business of Ferrets

A **ferret** is a domesticated version of the wild polecat, which animal is still to be found in the remoter parts of the United Kingdom, but which, unlike the **marten**, is not listed in *The Booke of St Albans* and the other early sources. **Ferrets**, which are mentioned in Pliny, have been used at least since the first century against rabbits and rats.

Alongside a **business of ferrets** is listed a **business of flies**. In *Lydgate*, at the end of the Caxton edition but not in the Wynkyn de Worde one, there appears a list of terms in which both are recorded. This difference rather emphasizes the fact that these lists were often used as 'fillers', in the same way that in many pre-war Penguins advertisements were used to fill blank pages and were not an integral part of the main text.

The old name for the polecat was a **foulmart** (pronounced foomart).

In *Henry V*, Act IV, comes: 'I'll fer him, and firk him, and **ferret** him.'

A Cabinet of Curiosities

When I read the entry in *Brewer*, a **collection of curiosities**, I was not much impressed, indeed I had decided to omit it from this book; I changed my mind, however, when I came across a somewhat similar entry in *Letters to the American Missionaries 1835-1838*, Cape Town, 1950. A circular dated 27 June 1838 begins:

> You are aware that there is, in connection with the Missionary Rooms, a **cabinet of curiosities**, collected principally by the missionaries of the Board.

The title of a 1992 novel by Allen Kurgweil is *A Case of Curiosities*.

A Cast of Hawks

Hodgkin comments: 'just as a **brace** and a **leash** were applied respectively to two and three grey hounds so **cast** and **leash** are applied to **hawks** of the tower.'

Emphasizing the difference of degree, so important in the Middle Ages, these terms were for use only with the **hawks** belonging to royalty, the nobility and the gentry. The **goshawk**, being a bird for a **yeoman**, was allowed only the term **flight**. *Porkington* thus allocates the hawks:

Ther havkes byñe of the tour
A garfavkon and a tarsselet A Garfavkon for a Kynge
A favkon jentyl and a tarsslet jetylle for a pryns
A favkon of the roche for a duke
A favkon perygryne for a norle
A basterd for euyry lord
A sakor and a sakorret for a knytte
A lannyr and a lanneret for a squyer
A marlyon for a lady
An hobby for a yovnge squyer
This byne havkys of the tour that fleythe frove the lur.

Chapman speaks out in his verse, loud and bold:

And as, on some far-looking rock a **cast of vultures** fight
Fly on each other, strike and truss, part, meet and then
stick by.
Tug both with crooked beaks and seres; Cry, fight, and
fight and cry.
So fiercely fought these angry kings, and shew'd as bitter
galls.

James Pilkington, sometime bishop of Durham, one of the

A Cast of Hawks

Protestant exiles who returned on Mary's death, wrote in his exegesis of the prophet Obadiah (in his use: Abdias): 'but among the popish priests ye shall find few but he can keep a cur better than a cure, can find a hare, keep a **kennel of hounds** or a **cast of hawks**, better than many other . . .'

Johnson quotes, in support of his definition, 'A **flight**; a number of **hawkes** dismissed from the fist', *Sidney*'s 'A **cast of merlins** there was besides...'

A **cast** usually refers to two hawks. Richard Blome, in *Hawking and Falconry*, speaks of 'A **cast of hawks** are two' and under 'Partridge Hawking' writes: '...into the field with a **cast** or two of **hawks** and about six or seven **couple** of good ranging **spaniels**, and when a **covey** is sprung, to cast them all off at a time, which affords good diversion to the spectators.'

Spenser in the *Faerie Queen*:

As when a **cast of faulcons** make their flyght
At an herneshaw, that lies aloft on wing,
The whiles they strike at him with heedless might
The wary fowel his bill doth backward wing.

Cast can and does refer to other than hawks. *Malory*, for example, has: 'Two **cast of bread**, with fat venison baked quarter bread or ale made at one time', and in *Wright* the definition is **cast**: 'A handful or **throw of fish**' and quotes: 'They count **casts** or **warps**, til they come to thirty-two of these, which make their "lang hunder".' *Northall* (1896) for long hundred: 'Six score.'

Five score to the hundred of men, money, and pins;
Six score to the hundred of all other things.

and he quotes from *Teesdale Glossary*, 1849, iii:

Nails, quills, and eggs are still sold at six score to the

hundred. The statute Hen. III, *De Mensuris*, and the statute 31 Edw. III, st.ii, AD 1357, *de alece vendendo*, ordained that a hundred of herrings should be accounted by six score.

He also comments: 'Oranges are sold by the long hundred at most markets. In SE Worc. long hundred = 112 lb.'

Jamieson also has **cast**: 'A **cast of herrings, haddocks, oysters** etc., four in number.'

Wright also quotes from a *Guide to Cromer:* 'Two crabs are counted as one, the two being called a "**cast**".' (Cromer is a Norfolk seaside town famous for its crabs. I noticed the other day a fish restaurant in the Waterloo Road with 'Cromer Crab' on its menu.)

Cast can also refer to the number of **lambs** produced in a season and also to the second **swarm of bees** in the season from one hive (*Jackson*).

Holme has: 'An **eirey of hawks**, or a **cast of hawks**: 2 a **lease of hawks**, and three a **staff of hawks**'.

Catalogue

Catalogues are normally descriptive lists of objects, books, paintings, *objets d'art*, but the word can also be used of ideas or concepts. A letter to the editor in *The Times*, 1 March 1991, contains this: 'If the General Synod of the Church of England should add to its **catalogue of errors** . . .'

A Cete of Badgers

Badgers are admirable beasts; the iniquitous pastime of badger baiting, although illegal, still survives. It beggars belief that men should find pleasure in watching one animal being torn to pieces by another. One tends to think that rural sportsmen in the past were indifferent to animal suffering,

A Cete of Badgers

but, although in general this may have been so, there were exceptions. The Revd W B Daniel in *Rural Sports* (1801), Vol I, wrote:

> The baiting of **badger** with dogs is a cruelty usually confined to the vicious and inhuman, who delight in seeing an innocent animal surrounded by its enemies, and which, altho' torn from his haunts . . . defends himself from their combined attacks, with wonderful activity and effect.

Halliwell gives **cete** as a **company of badgers**.

Turbervile says, 'As for fox, badgere and other such vermine, you shall seldome see more than one of them at once, unless it be when they engendre and then their encrease is called a **lytter**.'

Some sources have a **cete of grays**, **gray** being the old name for the badger. *Daniel* quotes the 'old saying: "as grey as a Badger"'. The meaning of **cete** is not definitely known – it probably derives from **coetus**: a meeting, assembly or company.

In the *Standard*, 13 October 1886, occurs 'keeping what old writers used to call a **cete of badgers**'.

Chapter

The canons of a cathedral, together with the dean, form the **chapter** and are responsible for the administration and governance of the cathedral; they are also legally responsible for electing the bishop, after the Crown has told them whom they have to elect. No choice. *Webster* has: '**Chapter**, a community of canons or canonesses.'

In some of the military orders of knighthood – the Templars, for example – the knights were formed into **chapters**.

There are also **chapters of accidents** and **chapters of**

possibilities. T H Huxley, the famous opponent of Soapy Sam – Samuel Wilberforce, Bishop of Oxford – in the debate on evolution, wrote in *The Crayfish* (1880):

> If an uninjured crayfish is placed on its back, it makes unceasing and well-directed efforts to turn over, and if everything else fails, it will give a powerful flap with the abdomen, and trust to the **chapter of accidents** to turn over as it darts back.

In the *Evening Standard*, 31 January 1991, in a review of a theatre production, the critic wrote: 'the rest of the show, which had been put together like a **heap of accidents** . . .'

In *Emily Montague* (1769), the first Canadian novel – although its author Frances Brooke was English by birth, she was the wife of the Revd John Brooke the first Church of England clergyman in Quebec – comes **chapter of possibilities**. The novel is in epistolary form. In 'Letter LV to Miss Rivers':

> So my dear, we went too fast, it seems Sir George was so obliging as to settle all without waiting for Emily's consent: not having supposed her refusal to be in the **chapter of possibilities**.

A Charge of Curates

The early lists have a variety of terms for assemblies or companies of ecclesiastical dignitaries. In the works of contemporaries such as Chaucer and Langland, although the clergy and the members of the religious orders people their pages, there is little record of companies of them, but there are vivid comments on their character and behaviour. Elsewhere in this book, separately, there are entries for some of the terms – for example, a **bench of bishops** and a **chapter of canons**.

Other terms like the **charge of curates** are listed, but in the *OED*, if they are noted, and not all are, there are no references to their use. A **converting of preachers**, a **dignitie of chanons**, a **discretion of priests**, a **doctrine of doctors** (these would have been doctors of divinity), an **observance of hermits**, a **pontifica of prelates** and a **prudence of vicars**.

'There is', wrote Sydney Smith, 'something which excites compassion in the very name of a **curate**.'

A **curate**, technically, is a priest who is given **charge** of the **cure** of the souls of a parish; now the term refers to the priest or deacon who assists the rector or vicar.

A Charm of Goldfinches

One of the best known of collective terms, widely used and beautifully descriptive of the flock of birds that in autumn or winter gather round teazel and thistle heads, their gold plumage glittering in the sunlight. Investigation shows, or seems to, that **charm** is a corruption of **cherme**, **chyme** or **chirming** and referred originally to the sound that the birds made not to their appearance.

Skeat (East Anglian Words) under **chirm** has: 'the noise of birds, of children, sometimes of women', and quotes Milton: 'with **charm** of earliest birds'. Charles Kingsley wrote of 'a "charm of birds" but he meant the chorus of birdsong that greets the Spring', at least so averred Mr Stilwell in *Notes & Queries 2*.

Northall has: '**Charm**, a hum of many voices' and quotes: 'What a **charm** them children mek in school.'

Another name for the goldfinch was the **goud-spink** or **gold-spink**. In *The Craven Glossary* is the quotation from Douglas's **Virgil**:

The sparrow **chirmis** in the wallis clyft
Gold-spink and lintquhite fordynsmand the lyft.

See also a **proud showing of tailors**.

A Clat of Worms

Elworthy gives '**clat of worms**' as a **bunch of worms** having 'worsted drawn through them for **clatting** (catching eels)'. The *OED* also quotes this example.

A Clowder of Cats

One has to be careful when writing of **cats**; their supporters and owners are so fierce and possessive; the mildest of adverse criticism is likely to evoke a hail of hostility.

Clowder appears in the early lists; the *OED* believes it to be a variation of **cludder**, a crowd or heap.

Clowder is also used of **carles** (or **churls**). In the north of England, **tom-cats** were sometimes called **carl-cats**.

Other collective terms for **cats** include a **cluster of tame cattes**, a **dovt of wyld cattys (dovt = do-out)**, a **destruction of wild cattes** and a **glorying of cattis**. There is also a **kindle of kittens** and a **kendel of young cats**.

The obsession with **cats** stretches back to the Ancient Egyptians, unbroken; the Revd W B Daniel, in his supplement to *Rural Sports* (1813), tells the following story:

Dr Barker kept a **seraglio** and **colony of cats**, it happened, that at the Coronation of George I, the *Chair of State* fell to his Share of the Spoil (as Prebendary of Westminster), which he sold to some Foreigner; when they packed it up, one of his favourite Cats was inclosed along with it; but the Doctor pursuied his *Treasure* in a Boat to Gravesend, and recovered her safe. When the Doctor was disgusted with the *Ministry*, he gave his *Female* Cats, the Names of the *Chief Ladies* about the

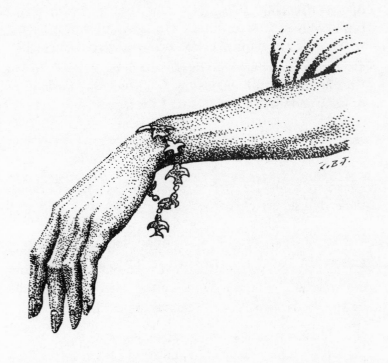

A Charm of Goldfinches

Court; and the *Male Ones*, those of the *Men in Power*, adorning them with the *Blue, Red,* or *Green* insignia of *Ribbons*, which the Persons they represented wore.

The colours are those of the orders of chivalry not of the present day political parties – blue was the colour of the Garter ribbon.

Dykes in Proverb XI, 'A **cat** may look at a king', comments: 'But a *fanatical* Puss in her *Majesty*, is a *dangerous* Creature, and fit for nothing but Don Quevedo's **Parliament of Cats**; and then they are all in a **Litter**, quoth *Lambert*.'

Cluster

Where we would probably now speak of a **bunch of grapes**, the early lists use **cluster**. Besides a **cluster of grapes** they also speak of a **cluster of nuts** and a **cluster of churls**.

Strutt on page xxx of the Introduction has **clusters of grapes** in a silver bowl; and *Grant*, a **cluster of kindred**.

In Spenser comes the line:

Her deeds were like great **clusters of ripe grapes**.

In Jonathan Gash's *The Great California Game* (1990) is the rather clumsy sentence: 'A **cluster of tourists** – so what was I? – went by, calling to each other.' One can imagine a group of earnest tourists **clustering** around their leader, waving phrasebooks and maps, 'hot for certainties' but destined to be given 'dusty answers'.

It would seem, following Bernard Levin's article in *The Times* (25 June 1992) and the ensuing correspondence, that the proper term for a collection of **twitchers**, those single-minded fanatics who like a pharaonic plague descend wax-coated and gum-booted wherever some small modest unsuspecting brown bird, having misjudged its usual route, has alighted for R and R★, is a **cluster**; also in *The Times* (21 July 1992), in its 'Life and Times' section, Neil Lyndon writes: 'I gave up my shotguns for a **cluster of reasons**.'

Marshall has a **cluster of turnips**; the glossary entry reads **clusters: crouds** or **clumps of turneps**.

Clutch

The number of eggs that a bird lays is called a **clutch**: a **clutch of pheasant's eggs**, for example. It is used sometimes to refer to the chicks once they have been hatched. See also **brood**.

One of Margery Allingham's later detective stories is entitled *A Clutch of Constables*; this, as the reader will discover, is a play on the word **constable**.

A new use, as I mention in the Introduction (see p.30), is to apply it – the occasions when this would be necessary are perhaps few, at least in polite society – to a collection or group of **phalluses**. Brian Aldiss in *A Hand-Reared Boy* (London 1970) refers to a **clutch of penises**.

A Coil of Teal

Walter Rye, in his 1895 glossary of dialect words used in East Anglia, includes a **coil of teal**. It is also recorded in the *Lonsdale Library*, where it says that **coil** is used for **teal** in the air. *The Booke of St Albans* has a **spring of teals**. *Hodgkin* remarks that rather than being a company term this is the term for the action of **teals** when flushed – they **spring** out of the water. *Wright* notes: 'Twenty or thirty **teal** in a "**spring**" or "**coil**" are seen.' See also **knob**.

Folkard of the **teal** says: 'they are generally to be met with early in the season in small **springs** of six or eight.'

★ A military term signifying Rest and Recreation.

A Company of Archers

A Column of Wild Duck

Walter Rye records: '**a column of wild duck**, a **string** or **skein** of them.' This descriptive term is applicable to birds in flight. There are, as those who consult this book (and its index) will discover, a great many terms that can correctly be applied to **wild duck** or **wild fowl**.

A Company of Archers

This is applicable to **bowmen**. **Company** was a term widely used in the Middle Ages. It survives today. *Brewer* lists **company of soldiers** and this is reflected in novels such as Scott's *The White Company*. In the *Book of Common Prayer* version of the *Te Deum*, there is 'the goodly **Company of the Apostles**'.

Dykes, Proverb XVIII, has:

> A **covey of partridges** in the *Country*, is an exact *Emblem* of a **company of gossips** in the *Town*. They have all the same *Calls*, the same *Haunts*, and the same *Basking-places*, for *junketing*, telling of *Stories*, and setting a whole *Neighbourhood* together by the Ears, with their Lies, Slanders, and Reflexions. *Gossipping Women* have the whole *Intelligence* of a *Parish*, and make a greater *Noise* in it, than the *London-Gazette*.

Folkard lists: 'a **company of widgeon** as the proper term to be used.'

A Conclave of Cardinals

Generally speaking, a **conclave** is or could be a meeting in secret of any group of individuals; but now it is used especially to describe the meeting of the **cardinals** of the Roman Church when they are walled up in the Vatican to elect a new Pope. When the waiting faithful see the puff of white smoke coming from the chimney, they know that a new Pope has been elected by the **Conclave** and the great cry goes up: *Habemus Papam.*

In *2 Henry VI*. Act I: 'I would the **college of the Cardinals** would choose him Pope, and carry him to Rome.'

A Confederacy of Dunces

The title of a book by John Kennedy Toole (1980). It is taken from a quotation from Swift's *Thoughts on Various Subjects Moral and Divers*.

> When a true genius appears in the world you may know him by this sign, that the **dunces** are all in a **confederacy** against him.

In *The Times, Saturday Review*, of 20 March 1992, there was a feature article by Julian Critchley on some of those MPs leaving the House of Commons. In the paragraph about Sir Robert Rhodes James this appears:

> He did not underestimate his own abilities either, but, sadly, they were never put to good use by his party. This could have been because he was never one of us; it is just as likely that the whips' office, sometimes a **confederacy of dunces**, could not recognize a good thing when they saw one.

A Congregation of Plovers

Plovers gather together during the autumn and winter, and those that migrate settle in great **flocks** to feed on the marshes and water meadows. In English terms **plover** refers principally to the green plover (that is the peewit or lapwing). *The Booke of St Albans* also gives a **desert of lapwings**, and earlier sources give a **deceit of lapwings** or **plovers**. This obviously describes the habit of the bird at nesting time of pretending to be injured in order to lure predators and others from the vicinity of their nests. *Hodgkin*

notes that the French country name for the **lapwing** is the
dix-huit, from its call, and that the word deceit may have
been intended as a *double-entendre* or a pun. Chaucer writes:
'The false lapwing, alle full of trechirie', and *Folkard*
explains that the bird is often hated in Scotland because, as it
is recorded in *Glossary to the Complaynt of Scotland*, 'it
frequents solitary places' and 'its haunts were frequently
intruded upon by the fugitive Presbyterians, during the
persecution which they suffered in the disgraceful and
tyrannical reigns of Charles the Second and James the
Second, when they were often discovered by the clamours of
the lapwing.'

Analagous perhaps is a **dissimulation of birds** – a term
common to many of the early lists. The *OED* defines it as a
'fanciful name for a company or **flock** of small birds'.

Macculloch (1824) has: 'A **congregation of fish** brought
together by means of a scatter of food; an angler's taking
advantage of the piscine convention over its diet of worms is
no more angling than a *battue* is sport.' *Bertram* (1873) also
has 'a **congregation of fish**'. Mr Parish in *Notes & Queries 2*
has a **wing** or **congregation of plovers** or **rooks**.

In *Hamlet*, there is a different kind of **congregation**. The
Prince says to Rosencrantz (Act II): '. . . the air, look you,
this brave o'erhanging firmament, this majestical roof fretted
with golden fire; why, it appeareth no other thing to me but
a foul and pestilent **congregation of vapours**. What a piece
of work is a man...'

In a letter that Brendan Bracken wrote to R A Butler,
when the latter was Chancellor, he said: 'I wish you a safe
journey to Turkey and hope you will not be lured to madness
in your **congregation of currency pundits**.'

A Convocation of Eagles

A Convocation of Eagles

Hellweg and *Lipton* both list this term, but I have found it in none of the old lists, nor is it in the *OED*. It is a mystery that so majestic and imperial a bird, from ancient times the symbol of power, should have no special term for its company. Perhaps there is one that I have yet to uncover.

Psalm 103, v.5: 'Who satisfieth thy mouth with good things; so that thy youth is renewed like the eagle's.' The explanation of this verse is that, rather like the phoenix, the eagle every 10 years immolated itself and was reborn. The *OED* for **convocation** has: 'An assembly of persons called together or met in answer to a summons'; thus in the past there were the **Convocations of Canterbury** and of **York**, which were the legal gatherings of the representative clergy of these two provinces and which are now but shades of what once they were.

Book titles, as a number of these entries indicate, are quite a good quarry for collective terms – Margery Allingham (see also **clutch**) used the title *A Cargo of Eagles* for one of her detective stories. On the World Service of the BBC (News Programme, 5 a.m. GMT on 11 March 1992), a commentator referred to 'a **cargo of misdemeanours**'.

A Coven of Witches

A **coven** is a gathering or a company of people; a **coven of witches** consists of thirteen witches and is based on the example of Christ and the twelve Apostles.

In Dylan Thomas's *Under Milkwood* there is a **coven of kettles**.

In Scotland in former times a **covin-tree** was the tree before a mansion at which guests were met and parted from.

A Coven of Witches

A Covert of Coots

It is not uncommon to hear it said that someone is 'as bald as a **coot**'; it is far less common to hear (indeed I have never heard it) a group of the birds described as a **covert**. Why this term is used it is difficult to say, for the bird neither hides itself nor conceals its nest; the latter, being an untidy pile of sticks and roots, is usually easy to find. The **coot** was regarded as a somewhat stupid bird; in Bale's *King John* comes the phrase 'no more wit than a **coot**', and in my childhood 'you silly **coot**' was a playground expression of derision. I have found in none of the old cookery books a recipe for its preparation, although *Folkard* remarks, he does not give its provenance, 'I do consider the **coot**, when dressed *à la Soyer*, a very wholesome and delicious bird'. Colonel Montagu's *Ornithological Dictionary of British Birds* (London, 1833) says: 'At this season [winter] of the year it is commonly sold in our markets . . . the flavour is rather fishy.' 'Coot shoots' are often held, their purpose apparently being either for sport or for the reduction of numbers rather than the replenishment of larder or deep freeze. There is, however, in *Swainson* a note under **Coot Custard Fair**: 'At Horsey, in Norfolk, a fair used to be held every spring called Coot Custard Fair because all the sweets were made from eggs of the coot and black-headed gull.' This is a note originally appearing in Stevenson's *Birds of Norfolk* (1866).

Mr Parish in *Notes & Queries 2* has a **covert** or **rasp of coots**, and the author of *British Field Sports* says that he has actually beheld upon the Manningtree river, in Essex, 'a **shoal of coots** reaching two miles in length, as thick as they could well swim, and half a mile over'.

A Covey of Partridges
Why a **covey of partridges** and not one of pheasants (a **nye**) or of grouse (a **pack**)? **Covey** has survived and is widely used and understood today.

Technically a **covey** is the **brood** of a single pair, the brood usually staying with their parents until the next mating period.

Richard Blome under 'Partridge Hawking', speaks of a **covey** – see above under **a cast of hawks**.

Earlier than *Blome, Harl 2* notes: 'And ye schall say I have fonde a **covey of pertrich**, a **beuey of quales** and **eye of fesauntes**.'

In *The Cold Yeare 1614, A Deepe Snow*, a contemporary tract that refers to the severe winter of 1613-14:

> . . . but if Angels doe fly, they have either their wings broken and fly not farre; or else are caught like **Partridges** a few in a **Couvie**.

Peachum in *The Beggar's Opera* says: 'I love to let women [e]scape. A good sportsman always lets the hen partridge fly, because the meet of the game depends upon them.' It is a keen-eyed sportsman who can distinguish the hen from the cock when in the air and at a distance. I do not think Gay could have been much of an ornithologist.

There is a proverb in *Bohn* that runs:

> If the partridge had the woodcock's thigh,
> It would be the best bird that ever did fly.

Gastronomically, I presume, not aesthetically. *Webster* also gives a **covey of girls** and attributes this to Addison.

A Cowardice of Curs
'Give a dog a bad name' – call a dog a 'cur' and man's best friend becomes a despised creature and its name a term of

abuse. What transforms Gelert from hero into villain? During my army service in India our camps were often plagued by **packs of pi-dogs** (at least that is how I spelt it in my letters home). These horribly unattractive creatures would haunt the camps and cantonments scavenging and copulating. When approached they would uncouple and slink away, the very embodiment of **cowardly curs**. Periodically sanitary squads would remove them – for ever. Probably in the medieval cities dogs like those were common, very different from the proud **kennels of hounds** of the nobleman.

Dykes in Proverb XXVIII comments: '**Cowardly Curs** always make the most *Noise* in the *Day-time*, and are loudest in the *Night*; whether a *Man*, or the *Moon*, or *Madness* be the *Occasion*.'

A Crash of Rhinoceroses

The first time I saw this used was in *Hellweg*, but in that book no sources for individual terms are given. *Lipton* refers to its use in an official report of the Kenya Game Department. It is expressive and apposite, as anyone who has observed these massive creatures can attest. It was in T S Eliot's play *The Confidential Clerk* that one of the characters is thus despatched:

> . . .
> Unfortunately, the father died suddenly ...
> *Lady Elizabeth*
> He was run over – by a rhinoceros in Tanganyika.

This conjures up the picture of a charging rhinoceros **crashing** down on its victim.

Crash is a new term that deserves to be used more widely; the older, more traditional, one is a **herd**. *Chambers*: 'The hunter was charged by a **herd of rhinoceroses**.'

A Crash of Rhinoceroses

In colloquial seventeenth-century English **rhino** meant cash; Cheatly in Thomas Shadwell's *The Squire of Alsatia* (produced 1688) says: 'My lusty rustic, learn and be instructed. Coal is, in the language of the witty [the underworld], money; the ready, the **rhino**. Thou shalt be **rhinocerical** [rich], my lad, thou shalt.' So perhaps a **crash of rhinos** could stand for **loads of money**.

A Credence of Sewers

One of the group terms dealing with servants. This one, according to the *OED*, refers to 'a company of sewers, or arrangers of dishes at table'. *Hodgkin* quotes from *Cowell* (1607): 'I have heard of an old French book containing the officers of the King of England's Court, as it was anciently governed, that he whom in Court we now call *Sewar*, was called *Asseour*, which cometh from the French *Assevir*, to set, settle or place. Wherein his office *in setting down to meat* is well expressed.'

Other terms include a **diligence of messengers**, a **kerfe of panters** – **kerf** was the act of carving or cutting up. *Hodgkin* says that 'the expression simply means that, if a "yonge gentylle man" wanted to use the proper term for the cutting of bread by the men-servants deputed for that purpose, he was to speak of it as a **"kerf of panters"**.'

An **obeisance of servants**, self-explanatory but probably sarcastic; a **safeguard of porters**, a **provision of stewards**, and a **seat of ushers**; this was not the schoolmaster **usher** but the overseer of banqueting halls, busy showing guests to their proper places and seeing that the food was properly served; now an occupation that has survived in those friends of the groom dragooned to wear ill-fitting hired morning dress and **usher** the guests into their proper pews in church.

Crew

Brewer in his list includes a **crew of sailors**.

In *The Political State*, Vol VII. 171¾ appears this Latin verse:

> Cedo, qui vestram Rempublicam tantam
> Amisistis tam cito?
> Proventabant oratoes novi,
> Stulbi, adolescentuli.

Which, for those denied the privilege and enriching experience of a classical education, was translated:

> How cou'd your State, so glorious once and great,
> In such short time fall to Contempt and Ruin?
> By a vile **crew of upstart politicians**,
> By hair-brain'd Boys and empty-noddled Speech-makers.

Webster's definition: an assemblage, is supported by a quotation from Spenser:

> . . . There a noble **crew of lords and ladies** stood on
>   everyside.

A Descension of Wodewales

The **wodewale** is the green woodpecker or yaffle. It is not easy to accept that **descension** is a company term for a group or company of **woodpeckers**. **Woodpeckers** are essentially solitary birds never moving in flocks. Much more likely, the term may refer to the undulating flight of the bird. *Halliwell* quotes the verse:

> I herd the jay and the throstelle
>   The mavys mevyd in hir song
> The **wodewale** farde as a belle
>   That the wode about me rong.

A Discretion of Priests

This, says the *OED*, is a fanciful term. It refers probably to the fact that everything that is **confessed** to a priest in the confessional is secret and must not be divulged to anyone else. One difficulty with the ecclesiastical terms used in the early sources is that the public's attitude to the Church was changing and descriptions that may have begun as compliments ended up as sarcasms. For example, a **devoutness of monks**, a **converting of preachers** or a **prudence of vicars**. There were other terms like an **observance of hermits** or a **doctrine of doctors** and a **pontifica of prelates** that are self-explanatory.

A Disguising of Tailors

This is a *Strutt* term which also appears in *The Booke of St Albans*. It refers to the ability of tailors to **disguise** or flatter a man by the clothes that they make, giving him, for example, wide shoulders or a noticeable codpiece. See also **a proud showing of tailors**.

A Disworship of Scots

In *Boorde*'s Letter VI, Leith, 1 April 1536: 'Shortly to conclude, trust you no skott, for hey wyll youse flatterying words, and all ys fal[s] holde.'

John Taylor, in *Christmas in and out* (1652), comments: 'and it is said that a Scot will prove false to his father, and dissemble with his brother, but for an English man, he is so cleare from any of these vices, that he is perfectly exquisite, and excellently indued with all those noble above said exercise.' On these no doubt biased and xenophobic sources the **disworship of Scots** is based. Dr Johnson observed that 'the noblest prospect which a Scotchman ever sees is the high road that leads to England', and in a conversation with Boswell expressed a less than enthusiastic view:

Boswell: I do indeed come from Scotland but I can not help it.

Johnson: That, Sir, I find is what a very great many of your countrymen can not help.

But there is some dispute about this term; **Scots** could be a misprint for **stotts** – the word that a number of the sources have. **Stotts** are **bullocks** or **steers**. It was an old custom that on Plough Monday, the first Monday after the twelfth day of Christmas, twenty men or so would yoke themselves to a plough in place of the usual plough **bullocks** and go round the village collecting largesse. If any house owner refused them, the team would plough the land in front of the house, thus showing this disrespect or **disworship** of the owner.

A Dopping of Sheldrakes

This term is used also of the **merganser** and the **goosander**. These birds all disappear under the water when feeding or when disturbed. In East Anglia **dop** is described in *Halliwell* as a short quick curtsey or bob, which accurately describes the action of these birds when on the water.

Sophronia, a character in Thomas D'Urfey's *The Richmond Heiress* (1693) says: 'Then at the Play-House ye ogle the Boxes, and **dop** and bow to those you do not know, as well as those you do.'

In *Notes & Queries 2* Mr Stilwell has a **depping of sheldrakes**, while Mr Parish has a **dopping**, and in *Folkard* it is recorded that: 'In the Outer Hebrides they [the **goosander**] are frequently to be met with in **doppings** of fifty and upwards.'

A Draught of Butlers

Whether this was a common expression it is hard to know.

A Draught of Butlers

Butlers in the Middle Ages occupied positions of rather greater importance than those of their counterparts today, who, when not decanting (or drinking) vintage port in their pantries, are busy despatching or depositing 'bodies in the library' – if the authors of detective stories are to be believed.

In *Amis and Amiloun, c.*1330 (EETS 203), these lines come:

> Sir Amiloun and Sir Amis
> He sett hem both in gret office
> In his court for to be;
> Sir Amis as ye may here
> He made his chef **botelere**
> In his court for to be.

Draught refers also to fish; there is in St Luke's Gospel the story of the miraculous **draught of fishes** (Chapter V). Mr Sparrow Simpson, *Notes & Queries 1*, in his answer to Dr Murray (see p.20 of Introduction) lists a **draught of salmon**.

A Drift of Fishers

The *OED* describes this as a 'fanciful name'. The recognized name for a fisherman's ground was a **drift**. The City Law (*Lex Londinensis*) 1680 states: '12 Item. That no fisherman or other shall presume to take up any rach or **drift** upon the water of Thames.'

Drift appears in a list of 'Terms used by Anglers explained' in *Daniel*, Vol 2: '[it] is a term when four or more Anglers are in company together, they are called a **drift**.' In the same list is: '**Leash of fish**, three.'

Bishop Hall in his *Contemplations* has: 'He that brought **armies of frogs** and **caterpillars** to Egypt can as well bring whole **drifts of birds** and **beasts** to the desart.'

A Drove of Beests

In some of the early sources, a **drove of nete cows** and **oxen**; it is easy to understand that it refers to cattle being **driven**, perhaps from the farm to the market or from the market to the slaughterhouse. It is similar to **drift**. *Halliwell* gives **drift** as '**a drove of sheep**'. *Hodgkin* also has **drift of tame swine**.

Lockit in *The Beggar's Opera* (1728): 'Lions, wolves, and vultures don't live together in **herds, droves** or **flocks**. Of all animals of prey, man is the only sociable one.' This ignorance reflects the extinction in Britain of the wolf and the absence of lions and vultures except as menagerie beasts.

Captain Boteler in *Recollections* (1805 to 1830) writes: 'While wandering in the woods a **drove of pigs** came by . . .' This was in the Baltic.

In *The Coral Island*, Chapter XI, comes: 'We found several more **droves of hogs** in the woods.'

A Druck of People

Dartnell & Goddard record this term as a Wiltshire description of a great **crowd of people**. *Wright* records it as a Somerset dialect word, and quotes: 'He likes his place in Church because there's not such a **druck of people** thereabouts.'

A Drunkenship of Cobblers

The *OED* notes that this is *The Booke of St Albans* entry for a **drunken company of cobblers**. *Hodgkin* (1907), reflecting the prevalent outlook of his day, writes: 'This is not a company of drunken cobblers, but only a habit that to this day is too prevalent amongst this class of workman.' Some early sources use two words, **drunken ship**, but this has not, I think, any great significance, pleasant though the thought is of **cobblers** behaving like present-day football fans on their way to commit mayhem on the continent.

Ray records a saying that reinforces the **drunkenship**: 'Cobblers and tinkers are the best ale drinkers.'

The Christmas Prince was a masque performed in St John's College in the University of Oxford in 1607 – printed in London in 1816. In the list of characters in 'Times Complaint', a part of the masque, one of them is 'Humphry Swallow, a **drunken cobler**'.

An Eloquence of Lawyers

One of the *OED* alleged terms. Its meaning, as *Hodgkin* says, is 'too self-evident'.

English barristers were grouped together in **Inns**. Today, **Gray's Inn** and **Lincoln's Inn** have survived, together with the **Middle Temple** and the **Inner Temple**, as the Societies to which barristers should belong – other **Inns**, for example **Clifford's Inn**, still exist in name and place but have no longer a legal function.

For legal affairs there were in the early lists a number of different terms: a **damning of jurors**, an **execution of officers**, a **sentence of judges**, and a **subtilty of sergeants**. Though to judge by the behaviour of Sergeants Buzfuz and Snubbins by Dickens's time the subtilty had disappeared. One of Chaucer's pilgrims was:

A **Sergeant** of the Lawe, war and wys
That often hadde been at the Parvys,
Ther was also, ful riche of excellence.

. . .

Nowher so bisy a man as he ther nas,
And yet he semed bisier than he was.

A shrewd comment. Lawyers today always seem busy, perhaps it is an excuse to boost their fees.

An Eloquence of Lawyers

An Embruing of Carvers

Embrue is a variant of **imbrue**. *Johnson* quotes a sentence from *Clarissa*, by Samuel Richardson: 'A good man chuses rather to pass by a verbal insult than **imbrue** his hands in blood.'

Chambers for **imbrue** gives 'to moisten or wet'. *Hodgkin*'s interpretation is this: 'It means literally making a mess with gravy or sauce. The term refers to careless **carvers**, splashing the gravy on the cloth whilst carving.' As the *Book of Keruynge* instructs its readers: '**Embrewe** not the table clothe.' *The Book of Curtesie* ascribed to John Lidgate has: '**Enbrewe** no napery for no rekelesness . . .'

A Fall of Woodcocks

An alleged name for a **covey** or **flight** of **woodcock** – *OED*. **Fall** is to be found in the early sources.

Hodgkin quoting an earlier writer:

> Consider their coming, which is so sudden (as to divers of the kinds) that *it is as if they dropped down upon us from above*. In **woodcocks** especially it is remarkable that upon a change of the wind to the east, about Allhallowstide, they will seem to have come all in a night; for though the former day none are to be found, yet the next morning they will be in every bush: I speak of the west of England, where they are most plentiful.

In other words, they **fall** out of heaven like manna or snow.

In Shakespeare's time the bird was trapped rather than shot – in *Hamlet*:

> Ay, springes to catch woodcocks . . .

and:

> Why, as a woodcock to mine own springe. Osric;
> I am justly killed with my own treachery.

And in *Twelfth Night*:

Now is the woodcock near the gin.

'In the time of the Elizabethan dramatists,' so *Swainson* tells us, 'tobacco pipes were often called "Woodcocks' heads", from their likeness to the bird's head and bill.' So Ben Jonson writes in *Every Man out of his Humour*:

Fastid: Will your Ladyship take any?
Savolina: O peace, I pray thee! I love not the breath of a woodcock's head.
Fastid: Meaning my head, lady?
Savolina: Not altogether so, Sir: but as it were fatal to their follies that think to grace themselves with taking tobacco, when they want better entertainment, you see your pipe bears the true form of a woodcock's head.

Brewer has a **fall of hair**.

Family
In the world of crime the **family** is a known concept, especially in America, but Vaux's vocabulary of the 'Flash' language (compiled 1812) contains this definition:

[**family**] usually refers to blood relations and relations by marriage but in the 'flash' language: 'thieves, sharpers, and all others who get their living upon the *cross* are comprehended under the title of 'The Family'.

In the same vocabulary: 'Cross, illegal or dishonest practices in general are called the *cross*, in opposition to the *square*.'

A Feast of Brewers
It seems, at least according to *Hodgkin*, that **feast** or **festere** was a mistranscription at some time of **sestere** or **sester**,

A Feast of Brewers

which was 'a wine or water measure containing 15 pints'. This shows, even as **charm** does in a **charm of goldfinches**, how a phrase changes through careless or ignorant copying.

A Fellowship of Yeomen

Riley shows that in a proclamation of Richard II the term the **Fellowship of Yeman** was used to describe what today we might call the Trades Union Society of **Yeman**, who in those times were sadlers' serving men. *Riley* also suggests that **yeoman** or **yoman** was probably the abbreviation of 'young man' and not an equivalent of today's **yeoman**.

Yeomen were in falconry assigned the **goshawk**; see under **cast**.

A Field of Racehorses

There is a story in a book of anecdotes published in 1794 about an Irishman. This man was much impressed – perhaps besotted would be a better word – by a racehorse called Botheram, which horse, for an important race, he persuaded many of his friends to back. The race started, away went the horses. Alas, it was soon seen that Botheram was last. 'Begorrah,' cried the Irishman, 'what a horse, see he's driving the whole **field** before him.'

There is also a **string of horses**.

A Fleet of Wild-duck

The Revd Mr Daniel in the supplement to *Rural Sports* (1813) relates many anecdotes. One of them is this:

An extraordinary occurrence took place, March 1810, near Drumburgh, a fisherman, placed a flounder net in the River Eden, which is subject to the flux and reflux of the tide, and on returning to take up his net, instead of finding fish, he found it loaded with wild-ducks; during his absence, a **fleet of these birds**, had alighted below the net, and on the flowing of the tide, were carried, from the contraction of the great impetuosity into the net, and were drowned. He caught one hundred and seventy **golden eyed wild-ducks**, supposed to be from the Orkneys, as very rarely any of that species frequent that part of the country.

A Flight

Flight, according to the *OED*, is the special term for a company of **doves**, **swallows** and various other birds. The early source has **goshawks**, **cormorants**, **doves**, **larks** and **swallows**.

Halliwell records it too, for the description of the 'first **swarm of bees**'. **Flight**, rather like **flock**, can be and is often used generally for companies of any bird in flight.

Proverb XVIII of *Dykes* (1709) is: 'Birds of a *feather* flock *together*;' in the reflexion on the proverb *Dykes* writes: 'But however the **proverb** be interpreted, it holds yet from a **Flock of Geese**, or a **Flight of Larks** (as wild as they are) to human Society and Friendship.'

Stonehenge lists a **flight** or **rush of dunbirds**. **Dunbird** is another name for the **pochard**. Mr Parish's list in *Notes & Queries 2* also has this entry.

A Fling of Oxbirds

Oxbirds are **dunlin**. This is a term that is listed by *Stonehenge*. The list comes in Chapter IX of the 16th Edition under *Wildfowl Nomenclature*.

Mr Parish's list in *Notes & Queries 2* also includes this term, but his entry reads: 'a **cloud** or **fling of oxbirds**'.

Lipton has: 'a **cloud of bats**', and in the Authorized Version of the Bible, Verse I of *Hebrews XII* runs:

Wherefore seeing we also are compassed about with so great a **cloud of witnesses**, let us lay aside every weight, and the sin which doth so easily beset *us*, and let us run with patience the race that is set before us.

Dorothy L Sayers chose this for the title of one of her detective stories.

A Flock of Sheep

A **flock of sheep** but not, strangely, of **goats**; **goats** are a **tribe** or, if wild, a **herd**. In St Luke's Gospel occurs one of the most famous and evocative of all Biblical verses:

And there were in the same country shepherds abiding in the fields, keeping watch over their **flocks** by night.

Flock is commonly, and *Folkard* would say wrongly, used for many species of birds. See Introduction p.17. *Coaten*, writing of Lord Rothschild's **pack of hounds**, says that it 'crosses the Vale of Aylesbury as a **flock of pigeons** cross a parish'.

A Fold of Highlanders

The vision of brawny, kilted clansmen, victims of the Clearances, penned at the docks awaiting transportation either to the colonies or across Hadrian's Wall to the fleshpots of England is a pleasing conceit but it would be wrong.

In *The Times*, 26 January 1991, it was reported: 'The Countess of Kintore was given her first Highland cow for Christmas 1972. Today she manages a **fold (herd)** at her husband's family home . . .

'Although prices have fallen in recent months, as with all beef cattle, a **fold of forty Highlanders** recently sold for an average of £1,400 per animal.'

Northall prints this rhyme:

He that would have his **fold** full,
Must keep an old tup, and a young bull;
He that would have a full **flock**,
Must have an old stagge, and a young cock.

A stagge is a gander.

A Fraunch of Millers

In *The Booke of St Albans*, but not in the *OED*. *Hodgkin*
suggests that **fraunching** means 'an insatiable appetite' and
quotes from Herman's *Vulgaria*:

He is ever fraunchynge
Revediae deditus est.

This could be a reference to the mill which is always hungry
for more corn to grind, and if one remembers Chaucer's
Miller and his tale, it could also refer to other more personal
characteristics:

His mouth as greet was as a greet forneys.
He was a janglere and a goliardeys,
And that was moost of synne and harlotryes.

A Fray of Fish

Mr W Sparrow Simpson in *Notes & Queries 2* – under a
sub-heading: *How fish are termed in companies* writes:

A **fray of fish** is the general term when many together.
A **scole of herring**
A **draught of salmon**
A **shoale of barbells**, or **beards**
A **bed of oysters, muscles** (*sic*) and **cockles**
A **flote**, or **troups of tunnyes**, or **whales**.

He takes this list from Randle Holme's treatise of 1688:
Academy of Armory and Blazon.

A Fold of Highlanders

A Gaggle of Geese

There are several terms for collections of **geese** besides a **gaggle: flock, wedge, skein. Gaggle** refers to domestic **geese** on the ground. 'Though their horses made magnificent bounds they all landed mid-stream and swam like a **gaggle of geese** in a field', *Coaten.*

Much earlier than *Coaten*, Reginald Scott in *Discoverie of Witchcraft* (1584): 'To make a **shoal of goslings**, or (as they say) a **gaggle of geese** to seem to draw a timber log, is done by that very means that is used when a cat doth draw a fool through a pond or river.'

Another word that can be used of **wild geese** in flight is **plump.** *Peacock* records: '**Wild duck** and **wild geese** are said to fly in a **plump** when they fly closely together.'

In a broadcast report of the Second Test Match at Melbourne, on 29 December 1990, the commentator, referring to some of the English team spoke of the '**gaggle of infielders**'. The whole English side for the series, save perhaps for the elegant and talented Mr Gower, could have better been described as a **collapse of cricketers**.

The early sources also use **gaggle** for a collection of **women** or **gossips.** *Dykes* in Proverb XVIII refers to a **flock of geese**.

A Gang

Brewer lists a **gang of slaves** and of **thieves.** *Chambers* and *Hellweg* record a **gang of elks.** The *COD* has **gang, company of workmen**, while *Chambers* also has 'a company of people banded together for a bad purpose: a **gang of thieves**'.

Under **gang**, *Dodington* has a **gang of poets, fiddlers, lovers** and **fencers.** We might add to this list 'courtiers'; the *Standard*, 26 March 1992, reports that Hugh Massingberd called the courtiers: 'a **farrago of toadies**'.

Lately in British politics four leading but dissident Labour politicians, David Owen, Shirley Williams, William Rodgers and Roy Jenkins, left the party to form the Social Democrat Party. Collectively they were known as the **Gang of Four**. Of that **gang**, as in the case of the Cheshire Cat, only the grin remains.

In a letter from a correspondent in California, *Notes & Queries 2*, occurs a **gang of wild turkeys**.

A Goring of Butchers

When this term was originally used, **butchers** killed their own meat; and it is easily understandable by anyone who has visited an abattoir or slaughterhouse how this term arose. It does not refer to butchers masquerading as unsuccessful matadors.

Hang

Walter Rye has an entry that records a **hang** as an alternative for a **crop**: 'a good tidy **hang of apples**', and *Wright* has an example of a Norfolk quotation: 'We've got a **rare hang of plums** t'year.'

Hang **refers** to fruit on the tree. One should not, however, while wandering round Harrods or one of the other large stores, use it to compliment the manager of the food department on his display.

A Harras (or Haras) of Horses

Halliwell's listing for **harras** has a **stud of horses**, – a stable, and quotes *Gy of Warwicke*:

> Than lopen about him the Lombars
> As wicked coltes out of **haras**.

In *The Times*, 24 December 1889, in a two-column article on the *Report of the Royal Commission on Horse Racing*, **haras** is used twice. 'The formulation of a **haras** ought to be accompanied, we think, by a scheme for providing liberal premiums for competition by Stallions . . .'; and: 'Other matters are dealt with in the report, such as the establishment of a Government **haras** or breeding station . . .'

Strutt for **colts** has a **rag of colts**, so does *Hellweg*. A **string of horses** usually refers to racehorses or hunters.

A Hastiness of Cooks

A fanciful name according to the *OED*; a sarcastic one according to *Hodgkin*: 'When one is in a hurry for something to eat it is well known that it takes the cook about twice as long to get the food ready.' Compare this with a **temperance of cooks**, a more widely recorded term. In ancient cookery, **tempering** referred to mixing with some liquid flavouring. It might, adds *Hodgkin*, also be a sarcastic term deriving 'from the not infrequent alcoholic propensities of otherwise first-class cooks'.

Johnson is reported in Boswell's *Life* of saying: 'Sir, we could not have had a better dinner had there been a **synod of cooks**.'

See also Introduction, p.25.

A Hatful of Medals

In a BBC report on the Winter Olympics – Radio 4 at 05.45 on 14 February 1992 – the announcer spoke of Austria winning 'a **hatful of medals**'. At the back of my mind there is a very faint recollection of 'hatful' being applied to something else, but at the moment I cannot identify what it is.

Heaps

Heaps is a word popular with the young and is used widely and loosely for: a great many, or plenty of. For example, 'Oh

A Hastiness of Cooks

Mum, there's **heaps of time**', when actually there is none! Although perhaps not strictly a collective term; in the *Evening Standard*, 4 March 1991, in that marvellous comic strip *Augusta*, Augusta being left with yet another 'Aunty' baby-sitter exclaims: 'We get through **heaps of aunties**'.

Herd

Herd is one of the most common and oldest of the terms used for collections of animals. Wiliam Twici, huntsman to Edward II, writes in *The Art of Hunting* (1307–27): 'How many **herds** of beasts are there? A **herd of harts**, and of **hinds**, of **bucks** and of **does**. A **bevy of Roebucks**. A **Sounder of Pigs**.'

Dame Juliana Barnes echoes this in *The Booke of St Albans*:

My chylde calleth **herdys of hert** and of **hynde**
And of **Bucke** and of **Doe** where ye hem finde.

Bishop Gawin Douglas in his translation of the *Aeneid* (1515) has: 'The **herd of hartis** with thar hedis hie.' And later, in 1674, Nicholas Cox, in *The Gentleman's Recreation*, writes of: 'a **Herd** of all manner of **Deer**'.

The early sources also indicate that it should be used for **curlews, cranes, swans, whales, wrens** and, strangely enough, **harlots**.

The **wren** in the Middle Ages was widely regarded as the king of birds. The legend is that it was decided that the bird which could fly highest would be king. The eagle soared into the heavens, far outdistancing all the birds – 'Look,' he cried, 'I am king.' But the wren, who had hidden himself behind the eagle's tail, fluttered a few feet higher and claimed and was given the kingship.

There was an old tradition in many parts of England that on St Stephen's Day (26 December) the young men of the village would kill a **wren**, then, carrying it on a bedecked pole, go round the village soliciting donations – asking for Christian boxes. This old verse from *Lean* records this:

The wren, the wren the king of the birds
St Stephen's was killed in the furze;
Although he be little his honour is great
And so good people pray give us a treat.

Folkard observes that: 'He who would get within range of a **herd of curlews** by daylight must be a cunning sportsman.'

According to the *OED* definition a **herd of harlots** was: 'a large company of people, a multitude, host. Now always in a disparaging sense.' A pity, perhaps, for it might have proved a useful term to use when explaining Shepherd Market and its environment and some of its more decorative inhabitants to innocent travellers from abroad. In the Middle Ages a **harlot** was not necessarily a woman of loose morals – *Jamieson* records that a **harlot** was 'a scoundrel, a worthless fellow', and quotes Chaucer: 'He was a gentil **harlot**, and a kind.' Camden thought that **harlot** was an aspirated version of Arletta, the mother of the Conqueror. William was widely recognized to be a bastard.

Herd is now used for companies of big game animals, **elephants, buffalo, zebra** and all manner of **antelope**.

An article in *The Times Saturday Review*, 16 May 1992, refers to **prides of lions** and **herds of wildebeest, gazelle, eland**, and **zebra** – as well as to **cohorts of zebra** and **carpets of vultures**.

When discussing **elephants**, *Topsell* (1607) writes: 'Also they never live solitary but in great **flocks**, except they be sicke or watch their young ones, and for either of these they remain adventurous unto death, the eldest leadeth the **herd**, and the second driveth them forward . . .'

A **flock of elephants** does not sound right. Certainly when I lived in East Africa we spoke of **herd**; **flock** was strictly for the birds. The arrival on one's lawn of a winged **flock of elephants** is a delightful if fanciful image – even were they to be pink.

Evans & Buckley referring to **porpoises** have: 'common round the coasts, either singly or in **herds**'.

Whitehead for a collection or **herd of hinds** has a **parcel**.

'It is also said', according to *Folkard*, 'that **cranes** used to assemble together before migration from our coasts; and thus, as if a proclamation had been circulated among the species, fixing a day and hour for the occasion of taking their departure, they rise high in the air in one entire **herd**; and having performed a few circumvolutions, dart off in apparently determined flight.'

A Hill of Ruffs

These are not the **ruffs** worn by choirboys and yeomen of the guard, but the male bird, *Philomachus pugnax*, the female is a **reeve**. *Stonehenge* includes this term in his 'wildfowl nomenclature', so too does Mr Parish in his *Notes & Queries 2* list.

Folkard also lists a **hill of ruffs** and says: 'At the present day the price paid for fattened **ruffs** is often as much as four guineas per dozen: almost as expensive as ortolans, and they are considered by some gastronomes as equally delicious.'

The *OED* definition is: **Hill** – rising ground on which **ruffs** assemble.

Host

This general term can be applied to a number of different things. The early sources list a **host of men** and a **host of sparrows**. It has also been applied to plants, witness Wordsworth's:

I wandered lonely as a cloud
That floats on high o'er vales and hills
When all at once I saw a crowd
A **host of golden daffodils**.

There is a **host of Angels**, as in St Luke: 'And suddenly there was with the angel a multitude of the heavenly **host** praising God . . .'

See also under a **murmuration of starlings**.

A Hover of Crows

Wilson records: 'a mile square **hover of crows** darkens air and earth.' This is a strange description, for carrion crows do not usually mass in such numbers, although I have seen as many as fifteen Hooded crows (the Scottish version) round a dead or dying lamb. A clue may be found in *Peacock* where it is recorded that in some localities **rooks** were called **crows**, in which case 'a mile square **hover of crows**' would not be impossible.

I have not found this term listed in the early sources.

A **hover of trout** appears in *Hellweg* and *Lipton*, but no provenance is given. In *Wright* there is an entry under **hover** which states: **Hover** – a hole in a bank where fish rest. It may be that this is whence the term **hover of trout** comes. *Elworthy* under **hover** has: Hiding place for fish. 'Any overhanging stone or bank under which a fish can hide is so called.'

Chambers and *Hellweg* have a **murder of crows**. I have found no reference to where this term has been used, but it is an acurate description of the behaviour of the Hoodie, as many Scottish shepherds will testify.

A Huske of Hares
There are several words for companies of **hares**, all of which seem to be rooted in the Middle Ages. Other terms beside **huske** are a **drove**, a **don** or **dun**, a **trace** and a **trip**. **Trace** appears in *Lydgate* and probably refers to the marks left by **hares** in the snow. *Turbervile* says, 'Also in time of snow we say the **trace** of an **hare**.'

In the appendix of *The Master of Game* there is a note: **huske**, a number of **hares**.

An Incredibility of Cuckolds
The exact origin of this is unknown, but one explanation, rather far fetched, is that in the Low Countries it was the custom in the later Middle Ages for the wool merchants to marry a second time, their first wives having expired from excessive and unrelenting childbearing. The young and buxom girls they then wed often found the lack of ardour of their husbands little to their satisfaction, and turned to the younger and more lusty apprentices, explaining to their husbands that they were teaching them the elements of good manners – their husbands happily forgetting that they had thus been taught, stayed in their counting houses and clubs where the rude would point to them and mock, calling them an **incredibility of cuckolds**.

A Kennel of Hounds
Kennels today are usually the places where dogs are lodged or boarded when their owners are travelling away from home. The Betjemanesque image of large, mannish, loose-tongued kennel maids clad in khaki breeches and with ample posteriors is one not uncommonly portrayed in those bucolic novels set in the Home Counties. This image I am assured, indignantly, is not only unacceptably sexist but also grossly inaccurate, kennel maids today are sloanes to a man. Orig-

A Huske of Hares

inally the term was used for the **pack of hounds** or **dogs** used for hunting.

The *OED* has: A **kennel of raches**

2 a **couple**
3 a **couple** and a half
16 a **kennel of hounds** or a **mute**
20 a large **kennell**

There is also a **sute of a lyam**. *Hodgkin* explains this as 'the following (suite) of a led hound'. **Limiers** are, according to a French source, 'chiens qui ne parlent point'. See also **brace**

Cox has: 'When the **relays** are well set and placed let the Huntsman with his pole walk before the **kennel of hounds**.' And again: 'A wolf will stand up a whole day before a good **kennel of hounds**, unless that **grey-hounds** or **wolf-dogs** course him.'

In the old poem 'Squyer of lowe degree' these lines occur:

To here the bugles there yblow
With theyr bugles in that place,
And seven score **raches** at his rechase.

Knob

A **knob** is sometimes used of a small quantity of **wild duck**. The *Lonsdale Library* definition is a 'small number of **pochard** in the water'.

The *OED* has a wider definition: 'A small collection of **widgeon, teal** etc.'

In his letter, *Notes & Queries 2*, Mr Salter mentions a **knob of widgeon** and various wild ducks. 'I have shot', he writes, 'the common **widgeon**, the **pochard**, and the **pintail** out of the same **knob**.'

Knot

Wright has: 'A cluster, group, company, a number of things.' He quotes Burns's poem 'Adoun Winding Nith': 'Yon **knot of gay flowers** in the arbour.'

In Gloucestershire a **knot of beasts**. Macaulay in Chapter 7 of the *History of England* (1849) writes: 'There was scarcely a market town in England without at least a **knot of separatists**. No exertion was spared to induce them to expose their gratitude for the indulgence.' This referred to James II's Declaration of Indulgence with which he sought to dispense with some of the requirements of the religious laws like the Test Acts that discriminated against Dissenters and Roman Catholics in favour of the Established Church.

One list, *Hellweg*'s, gives a **knot of toads**, but I have not found a reference to this in any early source. It may refer to the spawn, which unlike that of the frog, is laid in ropes or strings. According to *Evans* (1881), in Leicestershire toad spawn is called toods-tother.

Adams has: 'I have read that a string made out of wolves' gut put amongst a **knot of strings** made of the guts of sheep corrupts and spoils them all.'

Dodington has a **knot of astrologers**, and *Dykes* in Proverb XVIII: 'There is nothing more common here than to meet with a **knot of knaves** got together at *Nine-Pins* in publick, or at *All Fours* in private.'

Webster as an example of its meaning quotes Shakespeare (but no play title): His ancient **knot of dangerous adversaries**; and Tennyson (no specific poem): **knots of talk**.

A Labour of Moles

An alleged term according to the *OED*, but its possible genuineness is reinforced by Dryden in his translation of the *Georgics*.

The field mouse builds her garner under ground
For gather'd grain the blind **laborious mole**
In winding mazes works his hidden hole.

And George Herbert in *Grace* notes that:

Death is still working like a **mole**
And digs my grave at each remove.

The results of the **mole**'s labours, the piles of earth like crumbled chocolate that may disfigure a lawn, a green or a tennis court, can cause the owner or user mild apoplexy. The old word for a mole hill is a 'wonty-tump' ('wonty' pronounced 'oonty').

A Lack of Principles
When some years ago a group of former prime ministers gathered at No 10 Downing Street as guests of Mrs Thatcher the then incumbent, one of their number, Lord Callaghan, turned to Harold Macmillan and asked him what the collective noun for a collection of ex-prime ministers would be. According to Alastair Horne's written account in the second volume of his biography of Macmillan, he replied 'a **lack of principles**'. When I asked a friend, a Cambridge First, how she would write this she began L . . . A . . . K . . . H (the Hindu word for 100,000). So it could be a **lakh of principals/principles.** Will we ever know what Macmillan himself would have written?

Lipton has a **lack of principals**, but this suggests a shortage of institutional heads not a collection of anything.

A Lamentation of Swans
This sounds right but I have been able to find no written confirmation of its use. But, on 26 January 1991, along with several million other viewers, I heard and saw one of the

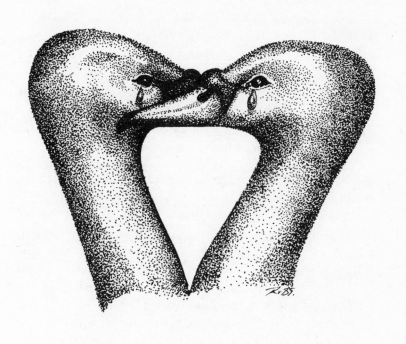

A Lamentation of Swans

detectives in the TV series *Inspector Morse* answer the question of a colleague concerning the proper term for a group of swans with: 'A **lamentation**, of course.'

The term obviously derives from the legend of the dying swan's last sad lament.

In the *Londsdale Library*, **swans** on the ground are called a **bank**.

In *Notes & Queries 2*, the term for an **assembly of swans** is a **whiting**. The love of special terms in the Middle Ages is shown in that lists exist for the proper descriptions for '**carving** and **sewing**' [serving]; for swans, for example, the term is **lift that swan**; for a **mallard, unbrace that mallard**; and for a rabbit, **unlace that coney**.

'The novice would be surprised as well as amused at the cracking and snapping noise made by a **herd of swans**, on rising from the water on a calm day.' And *Folkard* goes on to say that 'In Norwich they used to fatten swans for those who have swans and swan rights', and that when they are ready they are delivered with a recipe; this recipe was in rhyme, the final verse headed *The Gravy* reads:

> To a gravy of beef, good and strong, I opine
> You'll be right if you add half-a-pint of port wine;
> Pour this through the swan – yes quite through the belly
> To serve the whole up with some hot current-jelly.

A Laughter of Ostlers

The **ostlers** here are not the men who look after the horses but rather the **hostelers**, the keepers of inns or hostels. *Halliwell* besides giving **hostellere**, an innkeeper, also have: 'The students in the ancient **hostels**, or small colleges at Cambridge and Oxford were called **hostelers**'; so it might be that **laughter** refers to these students rather than to the innkeepers.

A Lavender List of Nominations

Strictly speaking this is not a legitimate collective term but it is a phrase that is now used and understood. When history passes her impartial and harsh judgement on the Wilson administration one of the few memorable things about it may well be the **lavender list**. It is the custom when a prime minister leaves office for those close to him or her, particularly those in the **kitchen cabinet**, to be rewarded with decorations or other honours. Mr Wilson's list, a somewhat idiosyncratic collection of political nominees, which at the time gave rise to a certain amount of adverse and serious criticism as well as bar-room ribaldry, was said to have been written on lavender-coloured writing paper, hence the phrase.

When Mrs Thatcher was unceremoniously bundled out of office in 1990 the list of people to be honoured that she had prepared was widely referred to in the press as her '**lavender list**'.

A Lepe (or Leap) of Leopards

Unlike a **pride of lions** (*qv*), a **lepe** or **leap** is not in general use today and, except in the medieval lists, I have found no record of use. Leopards are solitary animals; they do not hunt in **packs** or **prides**. Like Kipling's cat, they 'walk by themselves'.

Leopards are royal beasts; they are on the arms of the English Kings: the Leopards of England.

A Load of Kinnocks

This phrase was used by Michael Heseltine – then Secretary of State for the Environment – in a speech during the General Election of April 1992. It was widely reported at the time both in the Press and on television. The meaning is clear to those aware of the phrase a **load of old cobblers**; it did not refer either to a car full of the Kinnock family or to the coachloads of supporters that followed the Labour Party Leader from meeting to meeting. The **cobblers** here are not those mentioned elsewhere in this work.

The life of this phrase may prove short, although it will be found in newspapers of the period and may flummox eager Ph.D students of the future; in fact 'Atticus', *The Sunday Times* diarist, began his column on 3 May 1992 with this paragraph:

> During the election, Michael Heseltine coined the phrase a **load of Kinnocks**, but these days Labour is a **load of Goulds**. Bryan Gould is standing for the leadership and deputy leadership; Gill Gould, his wife and secretary, is helping to run his campaign. Not to be outdone, John Smith [the other and ultimately successful candidate] has appointed Jeanette Gould as his campaign officer. She is the daughter of Joyce Gould the Labour official supervising the contest.

A Lock of Hay

Dartnell & Goddard record that in the eighteenth century a **lock of hay** was the term used for a small quantity of **hay**, and *Wright* defines **lock** as a 'quantity of anything, generally a small quantity'. Thomas Hardy in Chapter III of *Far From the Madding Crowd* writes: '"Ah, the hut!" murmured Gabriel "I gave ten pounds for that hut. But I'll sell it and sit under thatched bundles as they did in old times and curl up to sleep in a **lock of straw**".'

Wright also records a Suffolk use: 'The small heaps unto which peas are raked at harvest are called **locks**.'

And in Jamieson's *Dictionary* (1840) – a **lock of meal**, a small quantity of meal, so too in *Dinsdale*.

A Lying of Pardoners

'Alleged' is the comment of the *OED*. A **pardoner** was a dealer or seller of pardons and indulgences. Of the one on the pilgrimage to Canterbury Chaucer says:

> A voys he hadde as smal as hath a goot.
> No berd hadde he, ne nevere sholde have;
> As smothe it was as it were late shave.
> I trowe he were a geldyng or a mare.
> But of his craft, from Berwyk into Ware,
> Ne was ther swich another **pardoner**.
> ...

[He goes on, comparing him to the poor parson.]

> Upon a day he gat hym moore moneye
> Than that the person gat in monthes tweye;
> And thus, with feyned flaterye and japes,
> He made the person and the peple his apes.

He was, as Chaucer clearly implies, a crook; 'japes' here meaning tricks rather than jokes.

In the *Prologue* to the Friar's Tale, Chaucer also describes the **somonour**.

> That of a **somonour** may no good be sayd;
> I praye that noon of you be yvele apayd.
> A **somonour** is a rennere up and doun
> With mandementz for fornicacioun,
> And is ybet at every townes ende.

The sources have an **untruth of sompners**.

A Malepertness of Pedlars

This term appears in *Strutt* and in many of the early sources. *Cotgrave* says: '. . . **pedlars** be not all evil, but of an indifferent behaviour.' A characteristic that distinguishes

A Melody of Harpers

many of today's pedlars, although the purveyors of white heather at some of London's railway stations can be, if crossed, somewhat malepert.

A Melody of Harpers

The *OED* says of this term that it is 'the pretended name for a company of harpers'. Except in the lists, I have found no record of its actual use; it would seem likely that it is to the sound of **harpers** rather than the company or number that **melody** refers.

The early writers obviously preferred the music of the harp to that of the pipes, for the description of a **company of pipers** is given as a **poverty**. The pipes are not, I think, the **bagpipes**, unless of course it is a Northumberland term.

Mess

The *COD* gives the definition as a **'company of persons** who take meals together, especially in the fighting services'. This is not wholly correct; the Navy uses different terms. It is ironic perhaps that the officers of a **regiment** (in itself a company term) are sometimes known as **the Mess**. 'The **Mess** won't stand for that kind of behaviour.' It is used, too, by transference to describe the place where its members meet to eat. I remember being reprimanded one day in India when I (a wartime soldier) said that I would meet a certain major (a regular) in the **Mess** for a drink after a hockey match. 'No,' he said, 'you mean the ante-room, the **Mess** is where we eat.'

When one eats one's dinners at the Middle Temple the long tables are divided, invisibly, into **messes** of four; a long table seating, say, twenty will be divided into five **messes**, and it is *de rigueur* to speak to members of the **messes** on either side.

In one of the *Loose Ends* programmes (BBC Radio 4) in 1991, a collection of **iguanas** was described as a **mess**.

There is also a **mess of pottage** for which Esau sold his birthright.

This seems to reflect the entry in the *Craven Glossary*:

The number of *four* at an entertainment at an inn, where a stipulation was made for a party to dinner at a certain price per **mess**, or *meos*:
'You three fools lack'd me fool to make up the *mess.*'
Shakespeare. *Love's Labour's Lost.*

In Latimer's *Sermons*, Volume 1, p.161:

There lacks a fourth thing to make up the **merse**, which so God helpe me, if I were judge, should be *hangum fuum*, a *Tyburn tippet*, to take with him if it were the Judge of the King's Bench, my Lord Chief Judge of England.

Mob

Brewer gives a **mob of wild cattle**; in the West Country it has been used of a **herd of deer**.

Pope, in *The Dunciad*, writes of a **mob of metaphors** and elsewhere of 'a **mob of gentlemen** who wrote with ease'.

The term seems to have been transported to Australia where it means a **flock** or a **drove**. T Walker (*Month in the Bush*, 1836) writes of '**mobs of cattle**'. Later authors also use the term: C Barrett in *On the Wallaby* (1942) speaks of a **mob of tucker** – **tucker** a local term for food – and K Weatherby in *Roo Shooter* (1968) writes: 'a **small mob of wild pigs**, mostly white with black spots'. There are no native wild swine in Australia, they must be descendants of escaped domestic pigs – perhaps of that once popular variety the Gloucester Old Spot.

In Shetland they sometimes speak of a **mob** or **school of whales**.

Barrett also has: 'fairly large **mobs of foresters** may still be seen – up to forty or fifty animals, sometimes more'. A

forester is the local Australian name for the **great grey kangaroo**.

Philpson, who derives **mob** from *mobile vulgus*, quotes Henry Fielding (*Jnl* 13 June 1756): 'That very large and powerful body which form the fourth estate of the community, and have been long dignified by the name of "the mob".'

Walter W Skeat in *Notes & Queries 1* in answer to a query wrote in the 28 November 1985 issue:

> Curiously enough I have lately come to the conclusion that the word **mob** may be dated 1690. In 1690 I find **mobile** in Dryden's *Don Sebastian*, I.i. but in III.iii. of the same I observe that he has the form **mob**.

Also in *The Political State of Great-Britain*, Volume VII, London 171¾, p. 186, there is an account of the arrest and the trial of three drummers of Her Majesty's Foot-Guards who beat their drums illegally and tactlessly (Queen Anne not being dead) at a demonstration in favour of the 'most illustrious House of Hanover'. The reporter writes: 'I'm inform'd that it appearing that the three *Drummers* before mention'd had accidentally gone along with the **Mobb**, they were set at Liberty and Discharged.'

Wm Cobbett dedicates *A Grammar of the English Language* (1820) to Queen Caroline, observing: '. . . Royalty has, in the hour of need, no efficient supporters but the people.' In it (Letter XVII, para 181) he observes:

> Nouns of number, or multitude, such as **Mob, Parliament, Rabble, House of Commons, Regiment, Court of King's Bench, Den of Thieves**, and the like, may have pronouns agreeing with them either in the singular or in the plural number.

Caroline was the estranged wife of George IV; he refused to

allow her to be crowned.

Chesterton in *Heretics* observes:

> There are no wise few. Every aristocracy that has ever existed has behaved in all essential points exactly like a small **mob**.

A Multiplying of Husbands

How on earth did this term originate and how is it that it is to be found in so many of the early sources, albeit with no context? Save for some formidable (and rich) ladies like the Wyf of Bath:

> She was a worthy womman al hir lyve
> Housbondes at Chirche-dore she hadde fyve

and later Bess of Hardwicke, it was usually the men who had a **multiplicity of spouses**, for having worn out their wives through much childbearing they replaced them fairly quickly when a vacancy arose – at least if church monuments present a true and trustworthy record. It could, but I do not think that it does, refer to the occupation of those who, like the woman in the Gospel, 'had many husbands'. She was told to 'sin no more'.

Brewer's list has: **multitude of men**. In law more than ten.

A Murmuration of Starlings

Cecil Rhodes so missed **starlings** and **sparrows** when he lived at the Cape that he imported both species; the **starling** today is as much a menace and nuisance in Cape Town as it is in London and other British cities.

In *The Times*, 6 January 1938, a correspondent writing about **starlings** says, '. . . that **congregations of starlings** gravely damage woodlands is now incontrovertible . . . Great **murmurations of starlings** are often represented as a peculiar phenomenon of our times but Sir Thomas Browne . . . [noted the fact in his *Miscellanies*].'

A Murmuration of Starlings

Some early sources also have **chattering** and **clattering**. The former is also used of **choughs**, a bird once common round the coasts of Britain but now confined to a few places in the west. The **chough** in legend is supposed to embody King Arthur; but this is not reflected in the company term a **chattering of choughs**.

A Muster of Peacocks

This exotic bird was brought to Europe from Asia for food and decoration. It is thought that **muster** may be a corruption of *monstre*, and refers to the display of the tail. The term occurs first in the medieval lists and has survived. Washington Irving in 'Christmas Day', one of the pieces in *The Sketch Book*, writes:

> There appeared to be an unusual number of peacocks about the place and I was making some remarks upon what I termed a **flock** of them that were basking under a sunny wall, when I was gently corrected in my phraseology by Master Simon, who told me that, according to the most ancient and approved treatise on hunting, I must say a **muster of peacocks**. 'In the same way,' added he with a slight air of pedantry, 'we say a **flight of doves** or **swallows**, a **bevy of quails**, a **herd of deer** or **wrens** or **cranes**, a **skulk of foxes** or a **building of rooks**.'

Which book, I wonder, had Irving been reading?

Hellweg also has an **ostentation of peacocks**, which is self-explanatory.

Mr Busten in *Notes & Queries 2* suggests a **splendour of peacocks**, whether this is his own invention or whether he is reporting an actual use is not clear. The term for carving a peacock in Randle Holme's *Academy of Armory and Blazon* (1688) is **disfigure that peacock**.

Yeats in 'The Indian upon God' perhaps plays on *monstre* when he writes:

> Who made the grass and made the worms and made my
> feathers gay,
> He is a **monstrous peacock**, and He waveth all the night
> His languid tail above us, lit with myriad spots of light.

A Mutation of Thrushes

This appears in two of the early lists; it is a strange term and cannot really refer to a collection or **company of thrushes**. The writer of a letter published in Hardwick's *Science Gossip* (1 June 1867) asks:

> Is it a recognized fact amongst naturalists that thrushes acquire new legs and cast the old ones when about ten years old? A great many persons in the neighbourhood give what appear well-authenticated instances of this: one of a **thrush** belonging to a clergyman at Stanwix, near Carlisle, which was visited and examined by many when the change was going on . . .

Swainson reports this but does not comment.

A Mute of Hounds

Spelman (1664) in his glossary has *muta canum*; a **mute of hounds**; another entry gives **mute**: a **kennel** or **crie of hounds**.

Mute also appears in *Sir Gawain and the Greene Knight*;

> Thenne was hit lif upon list to lypen ye houndez.
> When all ye **mute** hym merged to-geder.

A Never-thriving of Jugglers

A **never-thriving** can be roughly interpreted as a **thriftless pack**; by the end of the reign of Elizabeth I when Puritans

A Never-thriving of Jugglers

were growing in number and influence the moral writers of
the time ranked **jugglers** with 'ruffians, blasphemers,
thieves, and vagabonds'.

Earlier in 1508 Barclay could write:

> **Jugglers** and pipers, bounders and flatterers,
> Baudes and janglers, and cursed adouteres.

In *The Comedy of Errors*, Shakespeare, reflecting his age,
wrote:

> They brought one Pinch, a hungry, lean-faced villain,
> A mere anatomy, a mountebank
> A threadbare **juggler** and a fortune-teller
> A needy, hollow-ey'd, sharp-looking wretch.
> A living-dead man.

Today, **jugglers** warrant a kinder, more friendly description, for they, even the ones dropping their clubs outside St
Paul's, Covent Garden, give pleasure to their watchers and
to themselves. Juggling is a pastime increasing in popularity;
indeed so is clowning, for which there are now excellent
courses. 'Clowns', wrote Margery Allingham in *The Beckon-
ing Lady*, 'are children without innocence, that's why they're
so awful, truly awful, and why only children and people in
childish mood think they're funny.'

A Non-patience of Wives
Listed but not explained; but women's impatience is proverbial. In one version of *de Bibbesworth* in the margin to the
lines:

> De dames direct la companye,
> Des onnes ausi la companye.

is added a note: **une jangle**. Perhaps the scribe, although he
should have been celibate, was suffering from a **non-**

patience of wives and was moved to record what he thought should have been the appropriate definition.

In *Proverbial Observations*:

> There is one good wife in the country, and every man thinks he has her, and the advice: commend a wedded life, but keep thyself a bachelor.

A Nye (or Eye) of Pheasants

Why an **eye of pheasants**? One interesting explanation comes in *Britten*: '**Eye** – nest, brood. "When you have found an **eye of pheasants**". Probably corruption of French **nid**, nest, by loss of **n**.'

In early medieval times the French influence in England – through the Norman Conquest – was strong, particularly in such fields as hunting and field sports, so the explanation may be accepted as credible.

Peacock also has: '**eye** – a **brood of pheasants**', and *Dartnell & Goddard* have **nythe**, a **brood**: 'a **nythe of pheasants**: always used by gamekeepers.'

A Pace of Asses

A common term in many of the early sources, originally **passe**.

The *OED* has **pace** – a **company** or **herd of asses**. *Halliwell*, too, defines the word as a **herd** or **company of asses**. This term, according to *Skinner*, should be linked with a **rag** or **rack of colts**. *Hodgkin* has: '**Rack** – the proper term to be used in connection with **colts** to express the same meaning as the word **passe** used in connection with **asses**.'

Mungo Park in his *Travels in Africa* (1799) writes of 'A **coffle of fourteen asses** loaded with salt'; **coffle** is also used of **slaves**. *Livingstone* has: 'One who drove his **coffle of slaves** from the interior to the Portuguese settlements'; it was a term commonly used in the States and occurs in

Webster. It is, I think, properly, more a description of what the asses or slaves were doing rather than a term of assemblage. It is derived from the Arabic *kafala*, a caravan.

Pack

Pack is a commonly used word for groups of animals. A **pack of wolves**, a **pack of hounds** are widely used today.

William of Malmesbury in his *History* recalls: 'Edward the Confessor took the greatest delight to follow a **pack of swift hounds** in pursuit of game.'

Cox has: 'No musick can be more satisfyingly delightful than a **pack of hounds** in full cry. To such a man whose heart and ears are so happy to be set to the tune of such charming instruments.'

And in the *Jungle Book* Mowgli's Seeonee **Pack** has its own hunting song which begins:

As the dawn was breaking the **wolf pack** yelled
Once, twice and again.

There is also a **pack of grouse**, a **pack of cards**, and a **pack of lies**.

In *Notes & Queries 2*, Henry H Gibbs writes: 'A **pack of grouse** does not correspond to a **covey of partridges**. We say a **brood of grouse**: but towards the end of the season the **broods** (or what remain of them) begin to **pack**, and one may see, but not easily come within shot of, large **packs** on the hill.'

Elworthy includes: 'A measure of weight or number: a **pack of teazles** is twelve "staves" of twenty "bunches"'; and 'An indefinite number or quantity: **pack of nonsense**. What a **pack o' rooks**. A **brood of black-game**, analagous to **covey**.'

The *Craven Glossary* has an entry a '**pair of cards**. This was formerly the name given to a **pack of cards**. "A pair of

Packet of Love Letters

cards, Nicholas, and a carpet to cover the table." This quotation from *A Woman Killed with Kindness*.'

Craven also has **pack**, collected **broods of moor-game**.

William Stubbs in a letter to J R Green in 1871 wrote:

> Froude informs the Scottish Youth
> That parsons do not care for truth.
> The Reverend Canon Kingsley cries
> History is a **pack of lies**.

Britten wrote in 1880: '**pack of cows**: a **dairy of cows**, or a **pack of cows** as the term is in Cheshire.'

Dodington lists also a **pack of lazy, droaning devils**, and *Gent*, a **pack of knaves** and a **pack of juries**.

Dykes in his comments on Proverb XVIII observes that: 'A **Pack of Rakes** at a *Tavern*, is as notorious as a **Pack of Cards** at the *Groom-Porter's*. All *Gamesters* like *Birds of Prey*, will be about the *Carcass* of a *Cully*.'

In his column in *The Times*, 10 June 1992, Matthew Parris reports the MP Patrick Cormack as speaking of 'a **pack of greedy voyeurs** on the make' – journalists and fellow members.

A Packet

Small objects are often collected together and sold in **packets**, hence a **packet of biscuits**, a **packet of Christmas cards** or a **packet of love letters**, but a **bag of sweets** or a **bag of apples**.

A Plump

Peacock notes that: 'wild ducks and wild geese are said to fly in a **plump** when they fly closely together'.

In *Wild Fowler* **plump** is listed for 'small numbers of **wildfowl**, say thirty or forty'.

Webster quotes: 'To visit islands and the **plumps of men**.'

A Plocke (or Plucke) of Shooturners

The Booke of St Albans but not the *OED* lists this term. A **shooturner** is almost certainly a **shoemaker** and a **plucke** was a wooden peg, one of the shoemakers' tools. Why a company of shoemakers should be termed a **plocke** or **plucke** is not obvious.

A Pod of Whales

This does not appear in the early sources, it seems to have come into general use during Victorian times when it appears in books on whaling.

Moby Dick: '. . . well one day we lowered for a **pod of four or five whales**.' In *Moby Dick* one also finds a **shoal of sperm whales**. The term is also in use today. On 29 September 1990 in a BBC Radio 4 broadcast, a naturalist describing the behaviour of killer whales off the Patagonian Coast said, 'the **pod of killer whales** comes a month before the seals'.

In an article 'Flotation to save the Whale' in the *Sunday Telegraph*, 23 December 1990, '. . . to monitor the well-being of his **whale** or **pod of whales**, as they are collectively called'.

Gam is also used for a **herd** or **school of whales**, to gam means to gossip. The word is often to be found in the log books of the old whalers. It can also be used of a **meeting** of whalers at sea: a **gam of whalers**. *Hellweg* and *Chambers* have a **pod of seals**. In *Evans & Buckley* comes: 'The **pilot whale** lives in very large companies . . . an immense **herd** was captured . . . in 1846.'

In *Notes & Queries 1*, Mr W Sparrow Simpson, quoting from Randle Holme's *Academy of Armory and Blazon* (1688), has: 'A **Flote**, or **Troupe of Tunnyes**, or **Whales**.'

A Pod of Whales

A Pool of Typists

One of the definitions of a **pool** given in *Chambers* is: 'a group of people who may be called on as required, e.g. a **pool of typists**'.

See Introduction, p.29.

A Portfolio of Shares

In the last century, my grandfather's brother, Uncle Reginald, at the persuasion, if not insistence of the family, spent much of his life outside Britain in Latin America. Among his activities he dabbled in stocks and shares, particularly in utilities. His sisters, succumbing on one of his visits to his charm and his golden tongue, invested unwisely, building up a **portfolio of Latin American shares**, with the result that from a comfortable competence my great aunts teetered on the brink of penury, from which they were rescued by my grandfather. Besides **stocks** and **shares**, loose drawings, prints or sketches kept together are often called a **portfolio**; commercial artists offer to show perspective buyers a **portfolio of drawings** or **illustrations**.

A Pride of Lions

A survival from the Middle Ages which is in common use today. Safari parks and wildlife programmes on the TV have provided the general public with many opportunities of observing **prides** at close quarters. In the medieval Bestiary, Christ is often compared with the lion: 'Christ is the **Lion** who descended from the hill and lighted here on earth.'

A comparison that has its counterpart today in the *Narnia* cycle of children's stories of C S Lewis, in which the saviour is the great lion: Aslan, son of 'the Emperor over the sea'.

Webster does not mention a **pride of lions**, but it does describe the camel as the **pride of the desert**.

A Proud Showing of Tailors

Why should there be two company terms for tailors? (See also **a disguising of tailors**.) The answer, I believe, may lie in the fact that **proud tailor** is a local name for the **goldfinch**. *Wright* and *Halliwell* both give **Proud Tailor**: a goldfinch; and *Swainson* lists the counties – Derby, Notts., Leicester, Somerset, and Northants. – where it is so called. Maybe the term is one referring to **goldfinches** rather than to the makers of clothes; and this term, that later became restricted to a few mainly Midland counties, was at one time in general use.

In an article in *Archaelogia*, iii, p.33, 1786, title 'Some Account of two Musical Instruments used in Wales', by the Hon. Daines Barrington, and read at the Society of Antiquaries meeting on 3 May 1770 this paragraph occurs:

> But is is not only from the name of musical instruments which cease now to be in use, that passages may receive illustration, but from obsolete appellations of some of our most common singing birds.
>
> In the first part of Shakespeare's Henry IV. Act III, Scene 3, Hotspur says to Lady Percy (whose name by the way was not Catharine but Elizabeth)
>
> | | |
> |---|---|
> | *Hotspur:* | Come. Sing. |
> | *Lady Percy:* | I will not sing. |
> | *Hotspur:* | 'Tis the next way to turn *tailor*, or be robin-redbreast teacher. |

> Now a **goldfinch** still continues to be called a **proud tailor** in some parts of England; which renders this passage intelligible that otherwise seems to have no meaning whatsoever.

A Raft of Waterfowl

Craigie & Hubert describe **raft** as a **dense flock.** Lawson's

Carolina (1709): 'Raft fowl includes all the sort of small **ducks** and **teal** that go in **rafts** along the shoar.'

A **raft** can also refer to a quantity of persons or things. Mark Twain in *Sketches New and Old* has: 'He had one measure him and take a whole **raft of directions**.'

And in the *Daily Telegraph*, 28 May 1991, in a description of a cricket match the commentator wrote: 'Tufnell's painful day reached the surrender stage with the arrival of Speight who hit him for a succession of fours in every direction with a **raft of drives** and **cuts** before his dismissal brought in the declaration.'

Dickinson in *A Glossary of Words and Phrases pertaining to the Dialect of Cumberland* (1878) has a **raft o' fwok**. Whether such phonetic representation would hold up today is perhaps doubtful; how should the following entry from the same *Glossary* be transcribed?

> An early Methodist preacher in Workington used to enlighten his hearers with 'Aa was as seun expect a swine to gang **arsewurts** up a tree and whissle like a throssle, as a rich man to git to heaven'.

A variant of the camel and the needle's eye! **Arsewurts** is, according to Dickinson, the Cumberland word for backwards.

Webster's definition for **raft** is: 'A large collection of people or things taken indiscriminately [slang US]' and as an example gives: 'a whole **raft of folks**'. *Webster* also includes **raft** which it defines as 'a promiscuous heap' and supports with the quotation from *Barrow* 'a **raft of errors**'.

In *Lipton* there is reference to a **rafter of turkeys**.

A Rage of Maydens

This is not a description of angry women storming Lambeth Palace demanding instant ordination to the priesthood; it

A Rage of Maydens

predates such displays.

According to *Halliwell*, his second definition, to rage means 'to romp or play wantonly'. Chaucer in 'The Miller's Tale' confirms this:

> Now sire, and eft sire, so bifel the cas
> That on a day this hende Nicholas
> Fil with his yonge wyf to **rage** and pleye
> Whyl that hir housband was at Oseneye.

The *OED* refers to it as one of the alleged terms.

A Rascall of Boyes

A **rascall** was a **mob** or a **rabble**. *Hodgkin* says: 'This is one of the few terms in the list applied to persons which are genuine collectives.' The term **rascal** was a term also applied to beasts other than the four beasts of venery and the four beasts of the chase.

Halliwell gives two definitions: 1. **Rascal:** A lean animal, one fit neither to hunt nor kill; 2. **Rascal:** Common, low, it is the translation of **commune** in Hollybound's *Dictionaire* (1593).

There is an interesting note in *Archaelogia*, Vol 3. In a paper read to the Society of Antiquaries, 9 April 1772, by Owen Salusby Brereton Esq and headed 'Extracts from a ms dated *apud* Eltham *mense* Jan 22 Hen. VIII' appears this entry:

> Cap.34 herald, minstrel, falconer, or other, shall bring to court any **boy** or **rascal**; and by cap.36 no one is to keep lads, or **rascals** in court, to do their business for them.

Vestergeus (1634) points out:

> As before I have shewed how the ill names of beasts in their most contemptible state, are in contempt applied unto women, so is **rascall**, being the name of an ill-

favoured, leane, and worthlesse Deere, commonly applied unto such men as are held of no credit or worth.

A Regiment of Women
John Knox's famous pamphlet in 1538 against Mary Queen of Scots was entitled 'The First Blast of the Trumpet Against the Monstrous **Regiment of Women**'. Since that time, particularly of late years, the term, which was aimed originally at Queen Mary and her companions, has been used in a more general way by those horrified by the growth of feminism.

Dodington, a little picturesquely, has a **troop of women upon the high-way of hell** and also a **regiment of hypocrites and usurers**.

Macculloch nearly three centuries after John Knox, and continuing in the Scottish tradition, quotes a proverb of St Columba: 'Where there is a cow there must be a woman, and where there is a woman there must be mischief.'

In *The Uncommercial Traveller*, Chapter III, Dickens has a running head: **Groves of Old Women**.

Susan Faludi in *Backlash*, London 1992, has **droves of female careerists**.

A Richess of Martins
The **martin** or **marten** is to be found in the forests and wooded parts of Britain; its numbers have of late been increasing.

Twici names three classes of animals that are to be pursued. *Strutt* reprints these:

> The first class, beasts for hunting (the hare, the hart, the wolf and the wild boar); The second class, beasts of the chase (the buck, the doe, the fox, the **martin** and the roe). The third class, which afford 'Great dysport' are the grey (the badger), the wild-cat and the otter.

Groves of Old Women

The skin of the **marten** was greatly valued; it was one of the three furs to which a queen is entitled, the others being those of the beaver and the ermine.

A Rout of Wolves

Wolves, it should be remembered, did not disappear from Britain until the seventeenth century. *Fleming* records them as extinct in Scotland by 1680 and in Ireland by 1710; they therefore feature quite prominently in the medieval treatises on hunting. The common term then was **rout**; this has been replaced by **pack**. Turbervile in his *Book of Hunting* (1575) writes that 'the same number [of swine in a **sounder**] serveth for a **route of wolves**'.

There is a story that the decline of the **wolf** in England was started by King Edgar in the tenth century, this is repeated in *Archaelogia*, Vol X, 1792, p.165:

That lascivious prince, King Edgar, who acceded to the throne AD 957 wanting to detect the fraud and treachery of Earl Ethelwold, his favourite and confident, in an affair of love, projected a match of hunting in those parts where the lady resided, as if such rendezvous were not uncommon, and took that opportunity to slay him. Edgar, moreover, ordered a general hunting, or massacre of the wolves in his kingdom, as related above [This refers to a note recording the decline of the wolf numbers in England from this date and happening].

Freeman-Grenville in his *Chronology* records:

959-75 Edgar, the pacific, usurper King of Mercia, on 1 October King of England.

Webster gives as an example: 'A **route of ratones**', which it attributes to *Piers Plowman*.

A Route of Knights

The entry in the *COD* for **rout** has: 'assemblage or company esp. of revellers or rioters'. The earlier use was for an assemblage of people or creatures, while later use tended towards revellers or rioters. Most of the earlier sources use it of **knights**, although *Femina* has:

> Aray seyht man of knyttys
> A **route** seyth man of **squiers**

Chaucer:

> But **nightingales**, a ful gret **route**,
> That flyen over his heed aboute,
> The leves felden as they flyon.

In his long poem *The Forrest*, Ben Jonson writes:

> The **rout of rurall folke** came thronging in,
> (Their rudenesse then is thoght no sinne).

In passing it is interesting to note the memorial tablet in Westminster Abbey reads: 'O Rare Ben Johnson'. The 'h' has since been dropped.

The later use is shown in Hood's *Miss Kilmansegg, Her Dream*:

> For one of the pleasures of having a **rout**
> Is the pleasure of having it over.

And in *The County Ball* (1839) by Praed:

> And now, amid that female **rout**
> What scandal does he buzz about?
> What grand affair or mighty name
> Entrusts he to the gossip fame.

See also **rout of wolves**.

A Ruck of Stones

Nuthall says that in Warwickshire **ruck** is a heap or small quantity. There is (or was) a public house in Birmingham called the **Ruck of Bricks**.

The *OED* defines **ruck** as multitudes, large quantity, crowd, throng.

In *The Gentle Shepherd* (1725), Ramsey writes:

The spate may bear away
Frae off the howms
Your dainty **rucks of hay**

Stonehenge – 'When judgment is wanted in getting through a **ruck of horses**', and in a contemporary issue of the *Pall Mall Gazette* 'There is a **ruck of ambitious Gambettists** in the prime of life.' Gambetta was the French Premier in 1881/82.

Rush

Lonsdale has **rush** as the correct term for **pochard** in flight.

Mr Parish in *Notes & Queries 2* has a **flight** or **rush of dunbirds. Dunbird** is an alternative and earlier name for the **pochard**; *Stonehenge*'s entry is the same and so too is *Folkard*'s. The *Saturday Review* supplement of *The Times*, 16 May 1992, contains an article on travel in Tanzania; in it the writer comments: 'Montagu's harriers sailed overhead, and most poignant of all for an Englishman far from home, a **rush of swallows** sped over the grass.'

The *Scotsman*, 10 September 1901, has: 'The greater number of birds in the autumn **rushes**.'

According to *Wright*, **rush** can mean also a **cluster of plants**. He quotes from Richardson's *Borderer's Table-Talk* of 1846 – through a **rush of briars** and **nettles**.

School

There are **schools of porpoises** and **schools of whales**. **Whales** have a number of acceptable terms, all in use; a **gam**, a **pod**, a **shoal**; and all have impeccable pedigrees.

Evans reports: 'Professor Turner writes that in September 1889 a **school of dolphins**, nine or ten in number, has been chased off Hillswick.'

A group of **poker players** is sometimes called a **school**; so too are **artists** or **writers** belonging to a particular group that has a common approach or common values, for example the **Post Impressionist school**, or the **school of Raphael**, or the **Kailyard school** or in our own time the **Kitchen Sink school** (and what a boring **school** that one is!).

And, of course, there is the medieval **scole of scolars**.

Barrett writing of the **dolphin** says, 'they are beautifully shaped, slender creatures which associate in **schools** and prey upon **shoals of herring**'. They are today butchered and sold as tuna.

Vaux in his vocabulary of the 'Flash' language defines **school** as: 'a party of persons met together for the purpose of gambling'.

Mr Parish ends his *Notes & Queries 2* list with a **school of any wild-fowl**.

A Sea of Troubles

Hamlet in his oft-recited and memorable soliloquy speaks of taking:

> . . . arms against a **sea of troubles**,
> And by opposing end them . . .

Troubles, which a later and less remembered poet recommended should be packed up in one's old kit-bag.

School of Porpoises

A Sege of Herons

There is, according to *Hodgkin*, some confusion concerning the derivation of **siege**; he writes of the interpretation which he accepts: 'just as a commander lays **siege** to a "castelle" and, metaphorically, **sits** down until it capitulates or is taken or he is driven off, so does the patient **heron** stand at the waterside, or in the water, motionless for hours, waiting for the unwary fish to pass by and be caught.' *Blume* (1686) – two hundred years later than the first listing has: '**hern at seidge** is when you find a **hern**, standing by the waterside watching for prey . . .'

Sege appears in *Cox*'s list (1686) of falconers' terms, for **herons** were the legitimate prey of hawks and falcons; indeed eighteenth-century cookery books contain recipes for their preparation.

Appetites, like the meaning of words, change. Even were it allowed, few today would wish to eat **herons**. *Dolby* (1830) includes this recipe:

Heron (to roast). When the heron is picked, parboil it, lard the breast and back; roast it basting with white wine and butter beaten together; strew over it bread crumbs mixed with sweet herbs sliced small. Beat up the yolks of eggs with a little claret and vinegar, and some chopped anchovies. When roasted, serve it garnished with rosemary leaves, orange and lemon sliced.

Wentworth Day (1937): 'They are about in pairs instead of the "**sieges**" of half a dozen or more which one met only a month ago fishing on the tide line', and the *OED* quotes *The Islander* (British Columbia) of 5 June 1977: 'A **siege of herons** flying home against a sun set sky.' **Sege** is also used to describe a company of **bitterns**.

Sheaf

Halliwell's definition is a **bundle of arrows**. *Chambers* has: 'a **bundle** of things bound side by side esp. stalks of corn; a **bundle of** (usually 24) **arrows**'. Part of Chaucer's description of the squire's yeoman reads:

> And he was clad in cote and hode of grene.
> A **shafe of pecoke arwes**, bright and kene,
> Under his belt he bar ful thriftily,
> (Wel koude he dresse his takel yemanly . . .)

Sheaves of corn have vanished from most fields at harvest time; today the corn is threshed on the spot, and great **bundles of straw** are spewed out to lie in the fields like the broken columns of some monstrous straw temple long since abandoned.

In Hertfordshire fifteen **sheaves** used to be called a **shock of corn**. While in Kent, and some other counties, a **shock** comprised ten **sheaves**. *Lewis* also has: 'A **bolting of straw** is a quantity of **straw** tied up into a bundle or small truss.'

Skeat (Kenneth): '**Sheaf of arrows** was formerly a **garb of arrows**, which by the laws of Robert 1st, King of Scotland, was to consist of twenty-four arrows.'

Shoal

Moby Dick, besides its use of **pod of whales**, also contains a reference to a **shoal of sperm whales**. **Shoal** is used commonly of all manner of fish, **shoals of fish** in general or of a particular fish, **shoals of herring** or **cod** or **mackerel** are found in books, journals, newspapers, and in spoken everyday English.

Evans discussing the **gannet** records: 'Mr T Henderson, writing from Spriggie, says that during the time that the **shoals of herring** are about the land this species occurs in immense **flocks**.' *Skeat (Kenneth)* has a **cade of herrings**;

this refers to the number of dead fish – 'a **cade of herrying** six hundred, six-score to the hundreth' [720]. *Webster*'s definition is: 'a **cade of herrings** is 800, of sprats 1,000"; but *Craven* has: '(L. *cadus*), a small cask or barrel in which herrings are usually packed.'

In *Henry VIII*, Wolsey's sad soliloquy refers to another kind of **shoal**:

> And when I am forgotten, as I shall be,
> And sleep in dull cold marble, where no mention
> Of me more must be heard of, say, I taught thee,
> Say, Wolsey, that once trod the ways of glory,
> And sounded all the depths and **shoals of honour**
> Found thee a way, out of his wrack, to rise in . . .

Mr Parish in his list in *Notes & Queries 2* has a **shoal of rooks**.

Daniel, Vol 2, records:

> The grand **Shoal of Hadocks** comes periodically on the *Yorkshire* coasts. It is remarkable that they appeared in 1766 on the *tenth of December*, and exactly on the *same day* in 1767. These **shoals** extended from the shore near three miles in breadth, and in length from Flamborough Head to *Tinmouth* Castle, and perhaps much farther North-wards.

A Singular of Boars

The Booke of St Albans, when describing the names for swine of different ages, has this verse:

> And an hoggertere when he is of iii
> And when he is of iiij yere a **beore** shall he be
> From the **sounder of the swyne** then departith he
> A synguler is he so: for a lone he will go.

Hodgkin comments: 'A singuler is one boar, upwards of four years old.'

The term survived, for *Macculloch* (1824) writes:

> And this reminds me that Sky still contains a few deer, and, that although we have now nearly made the tour of the Highlands together, I have never named the nobel art of Venery in any of its forms; never spoken of a **singular of boars** or a **sownder of swine**, or a **sculk of foxes**, or a **gagle of geese**, a **murmuration of starlings**, a **sege of herons** or an **exaltation of larks**.

A Skein of Geese

The usual use today of **skein** is shown in a **skein of geese** or in a **skein of wool**. *G H Kingsley* has '169 **skeins of wild geese** clanking over our heads'.

Earlier, Whyte Melville, the underrated Victorian novelist and naturalist, in *Holmby House* (1850), a country novel of the Civil War, gives examples of **skein** in variations of both uses: '. . . lost in the long vistas of the park, threading the labyrinth by help of that delusive **skein** which we are pleased to term **history** . . .'; and: '. . . Patches of the undulating park were gilded with his beams: a **skein of wild fowl** disturbed in their quiet refuge down among the osiers, were winging their arrowy flight . . .'

The same book has a chapter headed a **Cast of Hawks** (*qv*) and records an old country saying which I learnt from our Cornish nanny: '"When the gorse is out of bloom, young ladies," quoth Sir Giles, "then kissing is out of fashion."' This saying, so we were assured, gave the speaker licence to kiss the woman or girl to whom he quoted it. It works.

Skulk

Thieves and **friars** join **foxes** under the term **skulk**. *Porkington* has:

a skolke of friers
a skolke of thewys
a skolke of foxys

Foxes are the raiders of hen houses and duck ponds; **friars**, in the climate of the later Middle Ages, were regarded as men of small moral probity and minimal religious conviction.

Evans (1881) in his *Glossary* has: **Skulk**, *sb.* one who shirks work. 'My employer, after he had discharged me, met me in public company, and called me a lazy, idle sculk. I, in return, called him a scamp, on which he wrung my nose.'

Tetzel, the seller of indulgences, against whom Luther delivered his cannonade of criticism, was a **friar**. The **friar**, travelling as one of Chaucer's pilgrims, was a man little respected by his companions. **Friars** were, with some justice, suspected of preying on the gullible and pious, the snapper up of many ill-considered trifles. The comparison with **thieves** is in need of no gloss.

Wright, besides giving **sculk** for a company of **foxes**, has: '**sculk**, an impure person'.

Three **foxes** are a **leash**, in *Daniel*, Vol 1:

In 1793, Sir Charles Daver's hounds found a **leash of foxes** in one cover, the hounds divided into three parts, each had a very severe run, and each killed their Fox.

A Slate of Candidates
This now refers primarily to the list of candidates for election put forward by a political party or special interest group. One would not usually describe all candidates as the **slate**, although I did hear it used in a report of the Democratic candidates taking part in a US Primary, but these were, although standing against one another, members of the same party.

Webster gives: 'A list of candidates, prepared for nomination for election.'

Slew

A twentieth-century American word meaning a **number** or **quantity**. It seems to derive from the old Irish **slog** – an army. In the *Evening Standard*, 22 April 1922, in an article on the wives of American Presidents, Eleanor Roosevelt's relations were thus described: 'Her father and brother were chronic alcoholics, as were a **slew of her uncles**. As a young girl, she had to triple-lock her bedroom when they were tipsily roaming the house.'

A Sloth of Bears

On a television quiz programme at the end of 1990 one of the questions was: 'What is a company of **bears** called?' The contestant did not know the answer, which the questioner then rightly read out – '**sloth**'.

In the Middle Ages many English towns had **bearpits** where **bears** were baited for the edification and amusement of the citizens. The last recorded mention of **bears** in the wild in the United Kingdom is given in *Fleming* as the middle of the eleventh century. In 1057 a man called Gordon is said to have killed a fierce bear.

Strutt, writing at the end of the eighteenth century, said:

> Bull and bear-baiting is not encouraged by persons of rank and opulence in the present day; and when practised, which rarely happens, it is attended only by the lowest and most despicable part of the people; which plainly indicated a general refinement of manners and prevalency of humanity among the moderns; on the contrary, this barbarous pastime was highly relished by the nobility in former ages and countenanced by persons of the most exalted rank; without exception even of the fair sex.

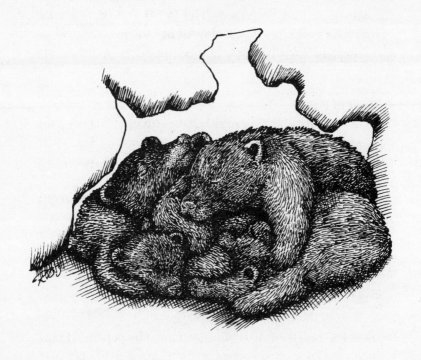

A Sloth of Bears

Macaulay observed perhaps a little unfairly but certainly memorably: 'The Puritan hated **bear-baiting** not because it gave pain to the bear but because it gave pleasure to the spectators.'

Performing **bears** were part of the travelling shows and fairs, and the ordinary people were used to seeing the great lumbering, seemingly clumsy, creatures either dancing at the end of a chain or being cruelly tormented in the **bearpit**; and their slowness would be observed, hence the word **sloth** – **slowth** in some listings. It is difficult to understand how the word came to be coined for a **company of bears**, for even in the wild great numbers neither congregate in the forests nor charge like the Assyrian on the herds and flocks of domestic animals.

A Sore (or Sorde) of Mallards

The **mallard** is the most common of the wild duck, the drake easily identified from the beautiful blue-green iridescent head and the duck by the flash of colour on the otherwise quiet plumage of the wing. The bird is almost certainly the main ancestor of the domestic duck with which it even now not infrequently breeds.

Halliwell gives '**sore**: a **flock of mallards**: . . . the term generally used in connection with **mallards** is **sort, sorde, sourde** from the Latin *surgere*, to rise'. *Egerton* has a '**flush of mallards**'.

John Skelton in *Merie Tales* (1567) reporting his harangue of his congregation says, 'And what be you (said Skelton) I say that you be a **sort of knaves** – yea, and a man might say worse than knaves . . .' A note says that a **sort** is a **pack**.

A Sounder of Swine

In his treatise on hunting: *The Master of the Game* (1406-13), Edward Plantagenet wrote:

> What men call a **trip of tame swine** is called of wild swine a **sounder**, that is to say if there be passed a five or six together.

Edward was the son of Edward III's son Edmund Langley, Duke of York.

The Booke of St Albans (1486) says:

> Twelfe make a **sounder of the wild swine**, 16 a **middle sounder** what place they be in, a **great sounder** of swine 20 ye shall call.

President Theodore Roosevelt, while still in the White House, wrote, in 1904, the foreword to the edition of *The Master of the Game*, published earlier in the century.

A Squat of Daubers

This does not refer to a semi-derelict house occupied by a commune of painters, paying no rent.

To **squat** is to bruise or make flat by letting fall, and this makes good sense if one remembers that a **dauber** was a craftsman who filled the timber frames of medieval and Tudor buildings with 'daub', puddled clay.

A Stalk of Foresters

Not **stalk** as in beanstalk, but as in the stealthy pursuit of one's quarry. This is another of the *OED's* 'alleged terms', but one which occurs in most of the early lists and which seemingly refers to the forester's occupation of **stalking**. Today, understandably but mistakenly, we are apt to think of foresters as tree people, engaged in the management of forests and plantations, whereas properly their work was akin to that of the present-day forest or game warden, responsible for the animals as well as the trees, as *Guillim* shows when he writes of 'Skilful Forresters and Good Woodman'.

A Stalk of Foresters

A Stud of Mares

A word widely used today. **Studs**, especially for **racehorses**, are apt to be found in many parts of the country. Archbishop Aelfric's *Vocabulary* gives 'Equastium Stood'. **Stud** has by association become a term of abuse or indeed envious admiration – it depends a little on the age and temperament of the user – and refers always to males. The *OED*: 'a man of (reputedly) great sexual potency or accomplishment'. *Nominale* has: 'a **stode of coltes**'.

Walter Rye, in his East Anglian *Glossary*, for **stud** has: 'a nickname given to a man for his love of venery'.

A Swarm of Bees

Swarm is the collective term for **bees**.

The Modern Husbandmen says:

> In a right year for their increase, there are many hives that have four **swarms**, that is from one hive a **swarm**, a **cast**, a **colt** and a **spew**. The **swarm** is the first and greatest number, the **colt** the next and the **spew** the least of all.

Lean has a saying: 'As thick as a **swarm of bees**', and also a poem from a *Shropshire Word Book*:

> A **play of bees** in May
> Is worth a noble the same day
> A **play** in June
> Is perty soon
> A **play** in July
> 's not worth a butterfly

Dodington has a **swarm of gawdy butterflie laquais**. I was fascinated when reading *The Beggar's Opera* to discover that in Air VI Polly Peachum sings:

Virgins are like the fair flower in its lustre,
  Which in the garden enamels the ground;
Near it the bees in play flutter and cluster,
  And **gaudy butterflies** frolic around.

Had Gay read *Dodington*?

Swarm can also apply to **wasps** and **locusts** and, if Gibbon is right, to **monks** as well: '. . . under their conduct a **swarm of monks** issued from the adjacent desert . . .'; earlier than Gibbon, the Elizabethan minor poet Barnabe Googe in his version of Thomas Naogeorgus's *Regnum Papisticum*, published in London in 1570 under the title *The Popish Kingdom*, has the line: 'Tell on good Muses for the **Swarmes of Monkes** doe yet remaine.'

Hone, 11 May 1826, 'A Warwickshire correspondent says that in that country "the first **swarm of bees** is simply called a **swarm**, the second from the same hive is called a **cast**, and the third from the same hive a **spindle**".'

John P Stilwell of Dorking, writing in *Note & Queries*, First Series, Vol VIII, 5 November 1853, says: 'In these parts the increase of the apiary is known by the three following names . . . 1st a **swarm** . . . next is called a **cast** . . . third . . . a **cote**.'

Webster records a **swarm of meteorites** and the quotation from Milton: 'A deadly **swarm of hornets**.'

Dartnell & Goddard: 'of **swarms**, only the first is a **swarm**, the second being a **smart**, and the third a **chit**'; and *Elworthy*: 'a **hive** or **swarm of bees** is always called a **butt**'; he goes on to quote a local saying as a very common expression: 'She would talk a **butt of bees** to death, she would.'

Daniel, Vol 2, has: 'destructive **swarms of locusts**, which in certain regions, have been sometimes known so to fill the Air as to obscure the light of the Sun . . .'

A Synod of Clergy

Just as there are special and different terms for groups of
geese on the ground and geese in the air, so are there special
terms for groups of **clergy**. There have been in the life of the
English Church great and memorable **synods** like the **Synod
of Whitby**, but those days are over. Today, the General
Synod of the Church of England contains not only elected
clergymen but laymen too: it is a body as memorable for its
mediocrity as it is for the effusion of ill-thought-out and
pompous opinions which too often issue from its delibera-
tions, destroying tradition and substituting promiscuous
arm waving and meaningless gobbledegook for decent seem-
liness and the clarity of Cranmer's prose.

See also under **hastiness of cooks**.

A Take of Fish

Brewer has **take**. Also in the *Daily Telegraph*, 25 June 1883,
'Small boats being used to ferry the **takes** to the smacks . . .'
Webster's definition is: 'The quantity of **fish** captured at one
haul or catch' and 'The quantity of copy given to a composi-
tor at one time.'

Team

Team is a word much used and abused by eager muscular
Christians and socialist ideologues; the former, blinkered by
ill-formed prejudice jettisoned the *Book of Common Prayer*
and traditional worship in favour of a collection of largely
insonorous platitudes and variations of the Mexican Wave,
and the latter, ever eschewing excellence, abolished compe-
titive sports, traditional marriage and grammar schools and
erected tower blocks of such inappropriate awfulness that
one is reminded that it was a **team of experts** that produced
a camel when designing a **horse**. *Johnson* has two definitions, the first: 'a number of **horses** or **oxen** drawing at once

the same carriage'; the second 'any number passing in a line'. In support he includes quotations:

From Shakespeare:

> I am in love; but a **team of horse** shall not pluck that from me, nor who 'tis I love;

and from Dryden:

> Like a long **team of snowy swans** on high
> Which clap their wings and cleave the liquid sky.

Team, like **herd**, is one of those general company terms that can be used for many different things, but, an important but, one has to be careful and one has to know when not to use it. Almost instinctively one recognizes that a team of foxhounds or a team of lions is inappropriate.

Other instances of use are to be found, for example, in *Gilbert White*: 'As to wildfowls, we have a few **teems of ducks** bred in the moors where the snipes breed', and in Spenser:

> A **teme of Dolphins** raunged in aray
> Drew the smooth charet of sad Cymoent;

Shakespeare:

> She is the faeries' midwife and she comes
> Drawn with a **team of little atomies**;

Pope:

> A **team of twenty geese** (a snow-white train!)
> Fed near the limpid lake with golden grain
> Amuse my pensive hours . . .

And in *Wright*: 'a **team of pigs**, a **good team of cows** and strangely perhaps a **team of links** – that is a string or chain of sausages.' *Skeat (East Anglian Glossary)* under **team** confirms this, he has: 'a string or chain of sausages is called a **team of links**'.

Analagous to the **team of oxen** drawing a wagon is a **team of huskies** drawing, to the cry of the driver, 'mush, mush,' a sleigh in the Arctic.

Lonsdale for **team** has a **brood** of young **duck** in flight; also of **swans** and **cygnets**; and Mr Parish's *Notes & Queries 2* list includes: 'a **team of ducks** on the wing'.

There is an article in *Archaelogia*, Vol 19 (1821), by Roger Wilbraham 'An attempt at a glossary of some words used in Cheshire' in which this entry appears: '**Chem**, or **Tchem**. s. **Team**, a **team of horses**, a **team of wild ducks**. Somner talks of a **team of young pigs**.' In the margin of the copy I consulted someone had written: '"teem", this, Ignorance!'

A Thrave of Thrashers

A **thrave of straw** was a **bundle of straw**. There is no unanimity; some say, *Wright*, for example, that a **thrave** was twelve or twenty-four sheaves of corn; others say two. 'It is also used metaphorically for a great number or huge collection of other objects.'

Bishop Joseph Hall in his *Satires* has:

Some drunken rhymer thinks his time well spent,
If he can live to see his name in print;

. . .

He sends forth **thraves of ballads** to the sale.
Nor then can rest, but volumes up bodg'd rhymes
To have his name talk'd of in future times.

A thrasher is a thresher.

A Throng of Angels

The eighteenth-century writer of hymns Nahum Tate wrote in his Christmas hymn 'While Shepherds Watched Their

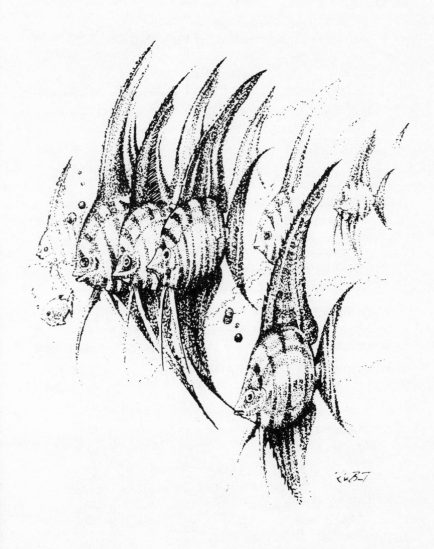

A Throng of Angels

Flocks by Night':

> Thus spake the Seraph, and forthwith
> Appeared a shining **throng of Angels** praising
> God . . .

Christina Rossetti's 'In the Bleak Mid-Winter' has a verse:

> Angels and Archangels
> May have gathered there
> Cherubim and Seraphim
> **Thronged** the air.

Dodington has a **throng of people**.

In a poem of Richard de Hampole quoted in *Archaelogia*, Vol 25, the couplet appears:

> When **throngs of knights** and **barons** bold
> In weeds of peace high triumphs hold.

A Tithing of Pies
Halliwell: '**Tithing**: a **company of magpies**'.

There are many rhymes about **magpies**; as children we were taught:

> One for sorrow
> Two for joy
> Three for a girl
> And four for a boy.

Other versions include:

> One for anger
> Two for luck
> Three for a wedding
> Four for a death
> Five for silver
> Six for gold
> Seven for a secret never to be told.

Campbell, in his *Life in Normandy*: 'Our Highland belief . . . the uneven numbers are unfortunate, and the even fortunate.' He also has a **congregation of magpies**, as well as a **shoal of trout** and a **flight of herons**.

Nowadays in the cities and their suburbs there has been an unwelcome explosion of the **magpie** population; not long ago I counted over fifty near the centre of Manchester; they are destructive birds preying on the eggs and young of smaller birds.

Tithing means **tidings**, as in: 'I bring you glad **tidings**.'

A Tok of Capercaillie
This appears in *Chambers 2*, but I have found it in no other reference book. The *OED* for **tok** says that it is an obsolete past participle for **take**. In the only Scottish dictionary that I found the word, a small tattered volume with no author, entitled *Dictionary of the Scottish Tongue*, fourth edition, Edinburgh 1827, it stated: '**Tok** – pret. **took**.' **Tok** is used, I think, in the way that **take** is used in the expression a **take of fish** (*qv*).

A Train of Mountebank – Apothecaries
This is one of *Dodington*'s terms translated from the Spanish. *Lean* records the saying: 'as **proud as an apothecary**'.

There is in the *OED* no record of this use.

A Trew Love of Turtles
The gift that my **true-love** sent to me on the second day of Christmas was '**two turtle doves**'. For **turtles** here are not the amphibian sources of Lord Mayoral soup but the **turtle dove** (*Turtur communis*), so named after its moaning song resembling the words 'turr-turr'. One of the most famous (and most beautiful) references to the **turtle dove** comes in the *Song of Solomon*:

A Trip of Goats

My beloved spake, and said unto me,
Rise up, my love, my fair one, and come away

For, lo, the winter is past, the rain is over *and* gone;

The flowers appear on the earth; the time
Of the singing *of birds* is come, and the voice
Of the **turtle** is heard in our land;

The ancients believed, wrongly, that **doves** mated for life:

As **true** as steel, as plantage to the moon
A sun to-day, as **turtle** to her mate.

(Troilus and Cressida)

They also believed, according to *Swainson*, that the widowed dove would never drink from any clear water lest its own likeness appearing on the surface should awake recollections of the mate it had lost.

Another term sometimes used: a **dule [dole] of turtles** emphasizes the mourning dolorous character of the bird. The **dove** is also the symbol of peace and of the third person of the Holy Trinity. The Holy Spirit, the Comforter, as the hymn says:

Come gracious spirit heavenly Dove
With light and comfort from above.

In the Celtic Church it was the wild goose not the **dove** that represented the Holy Spirit.

In the *Nominale Sive Verbale* under the section *Congregacio Auium* there is **un volec de columbes** (a **fligte of dowes**). What is perhaps a little strange is that in the same source in the section *La Noyse de oyseaux naturelment* the entry for the **dove** is *Columbe gerit Dowe Croukyth*.

Doves were kept in the Middle Ages almost as domestic fowls to supplement the winter food supply. Monastic and domestic dove cotes survive from this time.

Daniel, Vol 2, has a list of collective nouns which he says are in the language invented by sportsmen in the Middle Ages. This list, published in 1802, is almost exactly the same as that published by *Strutt* in 1810, but there is a difference – *Strutt* has a **dule of turtles**, while the earlier list has a **dule of turkies**. I can not but feel that this is a typographical error, all evidence suggests that it should be **turtles**.

A Trip of Goats

Widely listed in the early sources. *Turbervile* writes of a **trippe of goats**, and in the translation of the *Aeneid* (1515) by Gawin Douglas, sometime bishop of Dunkeld (this was before the Reformation), comes the line:

And **trippis** eik **of gait**, but any kepare.

Trip is also used of **tame swine, sheep** and **hares**, and *Lonsdale* has listed it for a **flock of dotterel** or for a small number of **wildfowl**. *Dartnell & Goddard*: 'A brood or flock, as "A vine **trip o'vowels** [fowls]".' Mr Parish in *Notes & Queries 2* has a **trip of widgeon**. *Jamieson* has: 'Then came a **trip of myce** out of thair nest', a quotation from Henrysone's *Evergreen*.

A Trogle of Snakes

In the key to 'Word-watching' in *The Times*, 30 June 1992, a **trogle of snakes** was defined as a 'bunch of snakes from the Greek *trogle* a hole' and the quotation cited:

Blue-scaled snakes rolled coil on coil,
Their hatchet heads hovering, the whole dark **trogle** alive
With rattling and hissing . . .

I could find no confirmation in the *OED*. When I wrote and asked him, Mr Philip Howard very kindly supplied the reference for the quotation. It is from Gardner's *Jason and Medeia*, New York 1973.

Troop

The *OED* defines **troop** as **herd, flock, swarm**, especially of **apes** and **monkeys**. The Australians sometimes talk of a **troop of kangaroos**.

Addison begins No. 130 of the *Spectator* (30 July 1710/11) with: 'As I was yesterday riding out in the fields with my friend Sir Roger, we saw at a little distance from us a **troop of gipsies**.'

In *Robinson Crusoe* (Chapter 20), Defoe writes: '. . . and on a sudden, we perceived two or three **troops of wolves** on our left, one behind us, and one on our front. So that we seemed surrounded with them.'

Tennyson in *The Princess* has the line: 'As flies a **troop of snowy doves** athwart the dusk.'

Troop is widely used today, not only in such general terms as a **troop of friends** but for special units in the army and in the Scouts.

A **troop of women** appears in *Dodington*, and in *Lodge*:

If thou see a **troupe of garded knaves**
Waite at Argastos heels like feriule slaves.

For **knaves**, *Strutt* has: 'a **nayful**, that is a **netful of knaves**'.

Alastair Cook in *Letter from America*, 3 February 1991, spoke of 'a whole **troop of congressmen**', and in *Tom Jones*, Book IV, Chapter 1, 'a large **troop** of half-a-dozen **scene shifters**'.

Daniel, Vol 2, in a passage on **shoals of herring** observes that 'The **dogfish**, which in vast **troops** assiduously attend the **herrings** wherever they go, carefully keep aloof from the great Mass of them.'

Hone's Every-Day Book, Vol 1, 1826 February 2, Col 203 has: 'Into this visionary she imagined that a **troop of virgins** came . . . then a **troop of young men**.'

A Truth of Barons

There are variations, caused one suspects by the inaccuracy of the scribes. The most common is a **thought of barons**. *Halliwell* and *Hodgkin* both agree that **truth** refers to the oath which **barons** swore to the sovereign:

> I become your liegeman of lief and lymme, and of earthelie worshipp; and Faith and Trowth shall beare unto you, to lyve and dye with you against all Maner Folke; so God me helpe . . .

Why this should be included as a company phrase in the old lists is difficult to determine, but they also include as company terms a **state of princes** and a **threatening of courtiers**.

A Trynket (or Trinket) of Cordwainers

A term not noted in the *OED*, but included in some of the early lists. A **cordwainer** is a shoemaker and a **trynket** was one of the tools used for cutting leather.

A **cordwainer** was a worker in cordovan leather which was imported from Cordoba in Spain, hence leatherworker or shoemaker.

An Unkindness of Ravens

'Who provideth for the raven his food,' asks Job, 'when his young ones cry unto God, they wander for lack of meat?'

In the Middle Ages **unkind** had the stronger meaning of 'unnatural' rather than that of lacking in kindness. *Swainson* says, '. . . ancient writers held the opinion that the raven was utterly wanting in parental care, expelling its young ones from the nest, and leaving them prematurely to shift for themselves . . .'

One of Ruth Rendell's crime novels is called *An Unkindness of Ravens*: it was lately (1990) turned into a TV programme.

A Wandering of Tinkers

A Wandering of Tinkers

In a number of the early sources **wondering** rather than **wandering**, but the correct term must surely be **wandering**.

Tinkers were in the late Middle Ages and Elizabethan period, even as they are today, not very highly regarded. *Harman* (1573) has: 'These drunken **tinkers** called also **prigs** be beastly people, and those young knaves be the worst.' Autolycus in *The Winter's Tale* was, 'Prig, for my life, prig! He haunts wakes, fairs, and bear-baitings.'

A Watch of Nightingales

Who has seen a **flock of nightingales**? Except perhaps if one has intercepted them somewhere on their migration, which certainly the authors and scribes of the early records would not have done. 'Nightingales do not", as *Hodgkin* says, 'sing in company.' He goes on: 'The word **wache** or **watch** is not in any sense a company term for a **flock of birds**, it is a term only used of a nightingale under certain conditions.' Yet in the letters in *Notes & Queries 2* correspondents record a **watching of nightingales** and a **watch of nightingales** as terms for an assembly of nightingales.

A Waywardness of Haywards

In the Middle Ages a **hayward** was an officer of the parish or of a township or manor and was responsible for keeping the fences and enclosures in good order. *Hodgkin* says, 'this term **waywardness** is probably only used because "wayward" rhymes with hayward'.

The *Craven* glossary has a different definition: 'a person employed to take care of the hay before stacked, as **woodward** is one appointed to guard or take care of wood.

The **hayward** bloweth mery his horne,
In everiche field ripe is corne.'

This quotation is from *Romance of King Alisaundre.*

A Wedge of Geese

This refers to wild birds in flight. **Wedge** is obviously descriptive of the formation in which the birds fly; it is also used of **swans**. The eighteenth-century logician Isaac Watts in *Logick* (1725) writes: 'The Robbers surrounded the coach: the **wild geese** flew over the Thames in the form of a **wedge**.'

John Ridd the hero of *Lorna Doone*, in the chapter 'Reaping Leads to Revelling', describes the actions of the workers: 'so like half a **wedge of wildfowl**, to and fro we swept the field'.

In *Stop Press*, a BBC 4 programme, the presenter said that the tabloids were 'far from being a **wedge of dying swans**'.

A Wilderness of Monkeys

Shakespeare in *The Merchant of Venice*:

> *Tubal*: One of them showed me a ring that he had of your daughter for a monkey.
>
> *Shylock*: I would not have given it for a **wilderness of monkeys**.

The term used in *The Booke of St Albans* is **shrewdness**, a **shrewdness of apes**. **Shrewdness** is one of those words that has, since the Middle Ages, changed its meaning. When it was then used it meant, as *Hodgkin* writes, 'wanton or malicious mischief'.

The poem *Robert the Deuyll* contains the lines:

> The elder he waxed, the more unhappye
> **Shrewdenes** he would do bothe in house and streate.

A Wisp of Snipe

Today a number of **snipe** in the air is quite commonly called a **wisp**. Traditionally the term is a **walk**.

Mr Parish's list in *Notes & Queries 2* includes a **wisp** or **walk of snipe** and in the same issue Mr Stilwell's list has a

walk of snipes; *Stonehenge* also has **walk** and so does *Folkard*.

In *Jamieson* for **to walk** the entry reads 'v.a. to **watch**', and quotes Archbishop Hamiltoun's *Catechisme*, 1552:

> Obey thame that hais the reule ouir you, – for thai **walk** for your saules euin as thai that mone gif a compt thairfor.

There are two different kinds of **snipe** found in Britain, the **common snipe**, which is a resident and is the larger bird; and the **jack snipe**, which is a regular winter migrant. Both make good eating. *Dolby* has a recipe. **Snipe** with truffles:

> Truss eight **snipes** with their beaks run through them, and roast them with bread under. Have a few truffles well stewed in a good known sauce and when the **snipes** are roasted [on a spit] lay them on the toast in the dish, putting one or two truffles into each **snipe**, and pour the remainder of the sauce over them.

Lean writes: 'The **jack snipe** is a very close lier.' Why is not immediately clear, for it does not, unlike the ringed plover, feign injury to lure the predator from the vicinity of its nest.

Neill (1806) writes of '**wisp of snipe**' and *Robinson* has: 'a barrel of shot emptied into a **wisp of larks**'. While a report in the *Aberdeen Journal* (1910) says, 'I had naething bit a **weesp o'eels** as the result of my fishing'.

A Worship of Writers
An alleged term from *The Booke of St Albans* for a **company of writers**; it appears also in some of the other early sources, but I can find it nowhere defined. **Poets**, according to *Dodington*, could be collected in a **gang**. It is unlikely that today one would seriously refer to Wordsworth or Coleridge as members of the Lake **Gang**.

A Worship of Writers

In *The Times* 'Diary' of 28 February 1992, the item headed 'Library Lobby' began 'A **shelf-load of writers** yesterday forsook their expensive garrets and assembled, blinking in the sunshine, outside the House of Commons to lobby arts minister Tim Renton over the underfunding of public libraries.'

For **painters** the term in the old sources was a **misbelief**, analagous no doubt to the **disguising of tailors**.

INDEX
AND
SELECTED BIBLIOGRAPHY

INDEX

Abnormal Importations,
   an armada of 34
Accidents
   a chapter of 15, 57
   a heap of 58
Adversaries, a knot of 103
Anatomy, an atlas of 36
Angels
   a band of glorious 37
   a host of 99
   a throng of 152
Antelope, a herd of 97
Apes
   a shrewdness of 163
   a troop of 159
Apostles, the goodly
   company of the 29, 65
Apothecaries, a train of 155
Apples
   a bag of 123
   a hang of 93
Archers, a company of 65
Arrows
   a bundle of 139
   a garb of 139
   a sheaf of 139
Asses
   a coffle of 120
   a herd of 120
   a pace of 120
Astrologers, a knot of 103

Atomies, a team of 151
Aunties, heaps of 96

Badgers
   a cete or set of 55
   a company of 57
   a litter of 57
Ballads, thraves of 152
Barbells, a shoal of 90
Barons
   a thought of 160
   a throng of 153
   a truth of 160
Bats, a cloud of 88
Bears, a sloth of 29, 143
Beasts
   drifts of 80
   a drove of 81
   a knot of 103
Bees
   a butt of 149
   a cast of 55, 148
   a chit of 149
   a colt of 148
   a cote of 149
   a flight of 88
   a hive of 149
   a play of 148
   a smart of 149
   a spew of 148
   a spindle of 149

Chickens
  a battery of 22, 48
  a flock of 48
  a peep of 48
Choughs
  a chattering of 116
Churls
  a chowder of 60
  a cluster of 60, 62
Clergy, a synod of 150
Cobblers, a drunkenship of
  81
Cockles, a bed of 90
Cod, shoals of 139
Colts
  a rack of 120
  a rag of 94, 120
  a stud of 148
Coneys, a couple of 47
Congressmen, a troop of
  159
Constables, a clutch of 22,
  63
Cooks
  a hastiness of 94
  a synod of 94
  a temperance of 19, 25, 94
Coots
  a covert of 71
  a rasp of 71
  a shoal of 71
Cordwainers, a trynket of
  160
Cormorants, a flight of 88

Corn
  a sheaf of 139
  a shock of 139
Courtiers, a threatening of
  160
Cows
  a dairy of 123
  a drove of 81
  a pack of 123
  a team of 151
Crabs, a cast of 55
Cranes, a herd of 96, 98,
  116
Cricketers, a collapse of 92
Crows
  a hover of 99
  a murder of 99
Cuckolds, an incredibility
  of 100
Curates, a charge of 58
Curiosities
  a cabinet of 51
  a case of 52
  a collection of 51
Curlews, a herd of 96
Currencies, a basket of 15,
  22, 39
Currency pundits, a
  congregation of 67
Curs, a cowardice of 72

Daffodils, a host of 30, 99
Daubers, a squat of 146

a stud of 93, 148
a team 151
Hostelers *see* Ostlers
**Hounds, foxhounds,
    greyhounds**
a brace of 46
a crie of 117
a couple of 46, 102
a kennel of 23, 54, 73,
    100, 102, 117
a lease or leash of 46
a mute of 102, 117
a pack of 23, 46, 89, 102,
    121
a relay of 47
Hunters, a blast of 41
Husbands, a multiplying of
    114
Huskies, a team of 152
Hypocrites, a regiment of
    131

Iguanas, a mess of 111
Infielders (cricketers) a
    gaggle of 92

Judges
the Bench of 40
a sentence of 82
Jugglers
a never-thriving of 117
a thriftless pack of 117
Juries, a pack of 123
Jurors, a damning of 82

Kangaroos
a troop of 159
see also Forester
Kettles, a coven of 69
Kindred, a cluster of 62
Kinnocks, a load of 107
Knaves
a knot of 103
a netful of 159
a pack of 123
a rayful of 160
a sort of 145
a troop of 159
Knights
a route of 134
a throng of 153

Lackeys, a swarm of 148
Ladies
a bevy of 20, 41
a crew of 76
Lambs, a cast of 55
Lapwings
a deceit of 66
a desert of 66
Larks
a bevy of 41
an exaltation of 141
a flight of 88
a wisp of 164
Lawyers, an eloquence of
    82
Lay Readers a convocation
    of 22

Syndics, The (Cambridge),
    43

Tailors
    a disguising of 77, 166
    a proud showing of 60,
        127
Talk, a knot of 103
Teal
    a bunch of 50
    a coil of 63
    a knob of 63, 102
    a raft of 128
    a spring of 63
Teazles, a pack of 121
Thieves
    a den of 113
    a gang of 92
    a skulk of 141
Thrashers or Threshers, a
        thrave of 152
Thrushes, a mutation of 117
Time, heaps of 96
Tinkers, a wandering or
        wondering of 162
Toadies, a farrago of 92
Toads, a knot of 103
Toasts, a superfluity of 33
Tourists, a cluster of 62
Troubles, a sea of 136
Trout
    a hover of 99
    a shoal of 155
Trustees, a board of 43

Tucker, a mob of 112
Tunnyes
    a flote of 90, 124
    a troop of 90, 124
Turkeys
    a gang of 21, 93
    a rafter of 128
Turnips
    a clump of 63
    a cluster of 63
    a crowd of 63
Turtle
    a dule [dole] of 155
    a true-love of 155
Twitchers, a cluster of 62
Typists, a pool of 29, 126

Uncles, a slew of 143
Ushers, a seat of 75
Usurers, a regiment of 131

Vapours
    a bunch of 50
    a congregation of 50, 67
Vegetables, a bouquet of 46
Vicars, a prudence of 59, 77
Virgins, a troop of 159
Voyeurs, a pack of 123
Vultures
    carpets of 97
    a cast of 52
    a drove of 81
    a flock of 81
    a herd of 81

SELECTED BIBLIOGRAPHY

Here, listed below, are some of the sources and books that I have used during the compilation of this work. In the text itself, the reader can see from the frequent references how much is owed to the late John Hodgkin; to the compilers of the *Oxford English Dictionary*; and to Dame Juliana Barnes's *The Booke of St Albans*; but perhaps not so obvious is the debt to those devoted and learned Victorians, members of the English Dialect Society, who recorded and thereby helped to save from oblivion many local words and expressions that otherwise might have been lost.

In this bibliography the name of the author is set in italic type. e.g. *Folkard*, this reflects the way in which the whole work is referred to in the main text by the authors' name only.

I

Manuscripts, those listed and quoted by *John Hodgkin* in his: *Proper Terms*, the supplement to the Transactions of the Philological Society, 1907–1910.

Egerton ms 1995
Porkington ms 10
Harley ms 541 – *Harl 1*
Harley ms 2340 – *Harl 2*
Addl. ms 33, 994
Robert of Gloucester ms. College of Arms
Digby ms 196. Bodleian Library
Gerard Langbaine's list in 'Junius'

II

Dictionaries

The Oxford English Dictionary. James A H Murray. Second edition prepared by J A Simpson & E S C Weiner. Oxford 1989.

Lucky indeed is the possessor of this work; a monument to Victorian civilization and scholarship.

Brewer, E Cobham. The Dictionary of Phrase and Fable. New and Enlarged Edition, London 1894.

A good wine needs no bush, nor a good book a free puff.

Chambers. Thesaurus, Edinburgh 1986.

Chambers. Twentieth Century Dictionary. Edinburgh 1977.

In my opinion, the most useful and comprehensive one-volume dictionary on the market; for the discerning reader.

Dolby, Richard. The Cook's Dictionary and House Keeper's Directory. New Edition, carefully revised. London 1833.

This contains some fascinating recipes for dishes that sound disgusting.

Gent, B E. A New Dictionary of the Terms Ancient & Modern of the Canting Crew in its Several Tribes of Gypsies, Beggars, Thieves, Cheats etc. London n.d.

Halliwell, James Orchard. A Dictionary of Archaic and Provincial Words, Obsolete Phrases, Proverbs and Ancient Customs from the Fourteenth Century. 2 Vols. London 1847.

Jamieson, John. Etymological Dictionary of Scottish. 2 Vols. Edinburgh 1808. Supplement, Edinburgh 1825.
   An abbreviated version of this marvellous work was made by J Johnstone and published in 1846.

Johnson, Samuel. Dictionary of the English Language. 2 Vols. London 1755.
   This should be required reading for every journalist and newscaster; but it is wise, if in doubt, to check definitions and entries against those in the *OED*. Not a book for the practitioners of political correctness.

Montagu, Colonel G. Ornithological Dictionary of British Birds. A New Edition by James Rennie. London 1833.
   Contains anecdotes and local names, and no small number of inaccuracies.

Skinner, Stephen. Etymologicon Linguae Anglicanae. 2 Vols. 1671.
   This work is in Latin.

Toone, William. Etymological Dictionary of Obsolete and uncommon words, antiquated phrases, and proverbs illustrative of Early English Literature. London 1834.

Websters International Dictionary of the English Language. The 1900 edition published in London.
   The latest contemporary edition of this standard work contains many new American words and expressions of unparalleled ugliness.

Wright, Joseph (Editor). The English Dialect Dictionary. London 1898.
   A mine of information.

Wright, Thomas. Dictionary of Obsolete and Provincial English. London 1869.

III

Glossaries, Vocabularies, and other sources.

Allde, Edward. Hawking, Hunting, and Fishing; with the true measures of Blowing. Newly corrected and amended. 1586.

Barnes or *Berners*, Dame Juliana. The Booke of St Albans. St Albans 1486.
   This is a most valuable source for many of the terms. Dame Juliana must have been a remarkable woman.

Barnett, Charles. An Australian Animal Book. Oxford 1955.

Bertram, G. The Harvest of the Sea. London 1973.

de Bibbesworth, Walter. Treatise of. A volume of Vocabularies edited by Thomas Wright. London 1857. The *Treatise* dates from the end of the thirteenth century.

Blome, Richard. The Gentleman's Recreation. 1686. Reprinted 1929.

Bohn, Henry G. A Handbook of Proverbs. London 1855.

Boorde or *Borde*, Andrew. The fyrst Boke of the Introduction of Knowledge. 1547. Reprinted E E T S. London 1870.

Boteler, John Harvey. Recollections of My Sea Life from 1808 to 1830. Publication of the Navy Records Society. Vol LXXXII. 1942.

Brant's Ship of Fools. Translated by Barclay in Barclay's Eclogues.

Britten, James. Old Country and Farming words gleaned from Agricultural Books. English Dialect Society. London 1880.

Campbell, W F. Life in Normandy. 2 Vols. Edinburgh 1863.
   A delightful Victorian travel book full of architectural and historical information – good on food, especially fish.

[*Carr*, Wm.] The Dialect of Craven in the West-Riding of the County of York, with a copious Glossary – By a native of Craven. 2nd edition much enlarged. London 1828.
   A pioneer work.

Chapman, G. Iliad. 1611. Iliad and Odyssey, ed. Shepperd. 1875.
   This is the book about which Keats wrote so memorably.

Cheetam, J. The Angler's Vade Mecum. 2nd edition. London 1689.

Coaten, A W. British Hunting. Lonsdale Library. London.

Cox, Nicholas. The Gentleman's Recreation 1674. Fourth enlarged edition 1697. Reprinted by The Cresset Press. London 1928.

Daniel, W B. Rural Sports. London. 2 Vols. 1801–2, Supplement 1813.
   A delight, the English country parson at his best.

Dartnell, George Edward & *Goddard*, Edward Hungerford. A Glossary of words used in the County of Wiltshire. English Dialect Society. London 1893.

Dickinson, William. Dialect of Cumberland. English Dialect Society. London 1878.

Dinsdale, Frederick. A Glossary of Provincial words used in Teesdale in the County of Durham. London 1849.

Dodington, J. The English version of the Visions of Dom Francisco de Quevedo Villegas. London 1688.

Douglas [Bishop] Gawin. Eneados. Edinburgh 1874.
   Douglas was a seventeenth-century Bishop of Dunkeld before the triumph of Presbyterianism; a man of many talents.

Drayton, Michael. Poly-Olbion. A Chorographicall Description of Tracts, Rivers, Mountains, Forests, and other parts of this renowned Isle of Great Britaine. London 1613.
   A detailed study of late sixteenth- and early seventeenth-century Britain. Well worth reading.

Elworthy, Frederic Thomas. The West Somerset Word-Book. A Glossary of Dialectal and Archaic Words and Phrases used in the West of Somerset and East

Devon. English Dialect Society. London 1886.

Evans, Arthur H & *Buckley*, T F. A Vertebrate Fauna of the Shetland Islands. Edinburgh 1899.

Fitzherbert, Master. The Book of Husbandry. Reprint of 1534 edition. Revd Walter W Skeat. London 1882.

Fleming, John. A History of British Animals. Edinburgh 1828.

Folkard, H C. The Wild Fowler. London 1859.
This work went through many editions and revisions during the Victorian period. It reflects the attitude of the traditional educated landowning class towards the encroachment and philistinism of the urban, liberal, confident businessman. See p. 17 of the Introduction.

Gent, R C. The Times' Whistle. Edited by J M Cowper. E E T S. London 1871.

Googe, Barnabe. English version of Thomas Naogeorgus's Regnum Papisticum published in London in 1570 under the title The Popish Kingdome or reigne of Antichrist.
Googe was an Elizabethan minor poet.

Grant, Ann. Essays on the Superstitions of the Highlanders of Scotland. 2 Vols. 1811.

Guillim, John. The Display of Heraldie. 1632.

Hall, Joseph. Virgidemiarum. The Three last Bookes of Byting Satyres. London 1598.

Harman, Thomas. Caveat for Cursetors. 1573
Hindley's reproduction 1871.

Hellweg, Paul. Weird and Wonderful Words. Newton Abbot 1986.

Helme, John. A Jewell for Gentrie. 1614.

Hodgkin, John. see under manuscripts I.

Holme, Randle. The Academy of Armory and Blazon. 1688. Roxburghe Club 1905.

Jackson, Georgina F. Shropshire Word-Book. Archaic and Provincial Words etc. used in the County. English Dialect Society. London 1878.

Lean, Vincent S. Collectanea. 4 Vols in 5. Bristol 1902–4.
A fascinating collection of sayings, proverbs, definitions, quotations, but often without attribution or source or date.

Lewis, [Sir] G C. A Glossary of Provincial Words used in Herefordshire and some adjoining Counties. London 1839.

Lindsay, Sir David. The Eight Interludes. Edinburgh 1786.

Lipton, James. An Exaltation of Larks. Harmondsworth 1977.
Lipton is the source of the title of this book: A Crash of Rhinoceroses.

Lydgate, John. The Hors, the Shepe, & the Ghoos. Caxton *c.* 1476. The Wynkyn de Worde edition *c.* 1499. Reprinted by the Roxburghe Club 1822. Edited by Sir M M Sykes.

Macculloch, John. The Highland, & Western Islands of Scotland. 4 Vols. London 1824.
This is a work to dip into if one has a love of Scotland.

Marshall, Wm. Rural Economies. London 1796.

Nominale Sive Verbale. Edited by Revd Professor W W Skeat. Transactions of the Philological Society 1903–6. London.

Northall, G F. A Warwickshire Word-Book. English Dialect Society. London 1896.

Notes & Queries 1. 6th Series XII. London 1885.

Notes & Queries 2. 8th Series 10. London 1895.
The great word masters of their age, Skeat and Murray, often used the columns of *Notes & Queries* to raise questions or explain definitions. See, for example, p. 20f of the Introduction.

Partridge, Eric. Slang, Today and Yesterday. London 1970.

Peacham, Henry the Younger. Compleat Gentleman. 1634. Reprinted Oxford 1906.

Peacock, Edward. A Glossary of Words used in the Wapentake of Manley and Corringham. English Dialect Society. London 1889.

Philipson, Uno. Political Slang 1750–1850. Lund 1941.
This is a work of Swedish scholarship.

Pilkington, James. Exegesis Obadiah, in works. Reprinted Parker Society. Cambridge 1842.

Pope, Alexander. The Odyssey. Methuen edition 1967.

Praed, W M. Praed Poems. Coleridge's edition. London 1864.

Ray, John. A complete Collection of English Proverbs. 1672. 5th Edition 1812 revised, corrected, and augmented by John Belfour.

Rye, Walter. A Glossary of words used in East Anglia. English Dialect Society. London 1895.

Skeat, Walter W. Reprinted Glossaries. Series B. London 1879.
———, A Glossary of Tudor and Stuart Words. Oxford 1914.

Spelman, Sir Henry. Glossarium Archaiologicum Henrico Spelmanno Equito, Anglo-Britanno 1664.

'*Stonehenge*', [J H Walsh]. British Rural Sports. London 1856.

Strutt, Joseph. Sports and Pastimes of the People of England. London 1801.
My copy is the Second Edition of 1810. It is beautifully illustrated and well printed. A mine of information.

Swainson, Charles. Provincial Names of Folklore of British Birds. London 1885.
Full of interesting and recondite facts. More accurate than Montagu.

Taylor, John. Christmas in and out. 1652.
This is a pamphlet published during the Commonwealth.

Topsell, Edward. Historie of All Foure-Footed Beastes. 1607 and enlarged 1662.

Triphook, Robert. Misellanca antiqua Anglicane. 1816.

Turbervile, G. The Noble Arte of Venerie or Hunting. 1576.

Twici, William. Le Art de Venerie (1307–27). The Art of Hunting, ed Sir Henry
Dryden. 1844.
Twici was huntsman to Edward II.

Vaux, J H. Memoirs, written by himself. 2 Vols. London 1819.
This includes the appendix: A New and Comprehensive Vocabulary of the Flash
Language. Compiled 1812.

Whitehead, G K. Hunting and Stalking Deer in Britain through the Ages. London
1980.

Wilson, O. Chronicles of Northumberland. London 1857.

Wright, Thomas. A Volume of Vocabularies from the Tenth Century to the
Fifteenth. Privately printed 1857.

ADDITIONS AND AMENDMENTS